Mometrix
TEST PREPARATION

DSST®

Money and Banking Exam Secrets Study Guide

I0893674

DEAR FUTURE EXAM SUCCESS STORY

First of all, **THANK YOU** for purchasing Mometrix study materials!

Second, congratulations! You are one of the few determined test-takers who are committed to doing whatever it takes to excel on your exam. **You have come to the right place.** We developed these study materials with one goal in mind: to deliver you the information you need in a format that's concise and easy to use.

In addition to optimizing your guide for the content of the test, we've outlined our recommended steps for breaking down the preparation process into small, attainable goals so you can make sure you stay on track.

We've also analyzed the entire test-taking process, identifying the most common pitfalls and showing how you can overcome them and be ready for any curveball the test throws you.

Standardized testing is one of the biggest obstacles on your road to success, which only increases the importance of doing well in the high-pressure, high-stakes environment of test day. Your results on this test could have a significant impact on your future, and this guide provides the information and practical advice to help you achieve your full potential on test day.

Your success is our success

We would love to hear from you! If you would like to share the story of your exam success or if you have any questions or comments in regard to our products, please contact us at **800-673-8175** or **support@mometrix.com**.

Thanks again for your business and we wish you continued success!

Sincerely,
The Mometrix Test Preparation Team

Need more help? Check out our flashcards at: http://MometrixFlashcards.com/DSST

Written and edited by the Mometrix Exam Secrets Test Prep Team
Printed in the United States of America

TABLE OF CONTENTS

Introduction

Thank you for purchasing this resource! You have made the choice to prepare yourself for a test that could have a huge impact on your future, and this guide is designed to help you be fully ready for test day. Obviously, it's important to have a solid understanding of the test material, but you also need to be prepared for the unique environment and stressors of the test, so that you can perform to the best of your abilities.

For this purpose, the first section that appears in this guide is the **Secret Keys**. We've devoted countless hours to meticulously researching what works and what doesn't, and we've boiled down our findings to the five most impactful steps you can take to improve your performance on the test. We start at the beginning with study planning and move through the preparation process, all the way to the testing strategies that will help you get the most out of what you know when you're finally sitting in front of the test.

We recommend that you start preparing for your test as far in advance as possible. However, if you've bought this guide as a last-minute study resource and only have a few days before your test, we recommend that you skip over the first two Secret Keys since they address a long-term study plan.

If you struggle with **test anxiety**, we strongly encourage you to check out our recommendations for how you can overcome it. Test anxiety is a formidable foe, but it can be beaten, and we want to make sure you have the tools you need to defeat it.

Secret Key #1 – Plan Big, Study Small

There's a lot riding on your performance. If you want to ace this test, you're going to need to keep your skills sharp and the material fresh in your mind. You need a plan that lets you review everything you need to know while still fitting in your schedule. We'll break this strategy down into three categories.

Information Organization

Start with the information you already have: the official test outline. From this, you can make a complete list of all the concepts you need to cover before the test. Organize these concepts into groups that can be studied together, and create a list of any related vocabulary you need to learn so you can brush up on any difficult terms. You'll want to keep this vocabulary list handy once you actually start studying since you may need to add to it along the way.

Time Management

Once you have your set of study concepts, decide how to spread them out over the time you have left before the test. Break your study plan into small, clear goals so you have a manageable task for each day and know exactly what you're doing. Then just focus on one small step at a time. When you manage your time this way, you don't need to spend hours at a time studying. Studying a small block of content for a short period each day helps you retain information better and avoid stressing over how much you have left to do. You can relax knowing that you have a plan to cover everything in time. In order for this strategy to be effective though, you have to start studying early and stick to your schedule. Avoid the exhaustion and futility that comes from last-minute cramming!

Study Environment

The environment you study in has a big impact on your learning. Studying in a coffee shop, while probably more enjoyable, is not likely to be as fruitful as studying in a quiet room. It's important to keep distractions to a minimum. You're only planning to study for a short block of time, so make the most of it. Don't pause to check your phone or get up to find a snack. It's also important to **avoid multitasking**. Research has consistently shown that multitasking will make your studying dramatically less effective. Your study area should also be comfortable and well-lit so you don't have the distraction of straining your eyes or sitting on an uncomfortable chair.

The time of day you study is also important. You want to be rested and alert. Don't wait until just before bedtime. Study when you'll be most likely to comprehend and remember. Even better, if you know what time of day your test will be, set that time aside for study. That way your brain will be used to working on that subject at that specific time and you'll have a better chance of recalling information.

Finally, it can be helpful to team up with others who are studying for the same test. Your actual studying should be done in as isolated an environment as possible, but the work of organizing the information and setting up the study plan can be divided up. In between study sessions, you can discuss with your teammates the concepts that you're all studying and quiz each other on the details. Just be sure that your teammates are as serious about the test as you are. If you find that your study time is being replaced with social time, you might need to find a new team.

Secret Key #2 – Make Your Studying Count

You're devoting a lot of time and effort to preparing for this test, so you want to be absolutely certain it will pay off. This means doing more than just reading the content and hoping you can remember it on test day. It's important to make every minute of study count. There are two main areas you can focus on to make your studying count.

Retention

It doesn't matter how much time you study if you can't remember the material. You need to make sure you are retaining the concepts. To check your retention of the information you're learning, try recalling it at later times with minimal prompting. Try carrying around flashcards and glance at one or two from time to time or ask a friend who's also studying for the test to quiz you.

To enhance your retention, look for ways to put the information into practice so that you can apply it rather than simply recalling it. If you're using the information in practical ways, it will be much easier to remember. Similarly, it helps to solidify a concept in your mind if you're not only reading it to yourself but also explaining it to someone else. Ask a friend to let you teach them about a concept you're a little shaky on (or speak aloud to an imaginary audience if necessary). As you try to summarize, define, give examples, and answer your friend's questions, you'll understand the concepts better and they will stay with you longer. Finally, step back for a big picture view and ask yourself how each piece of information fits with the whole subject. When you link the different concepts together and see them working together as a whole, it's easier to remember the individual components.

Finally, practice showing your work on any multi-step problems, even if you're just studying. Writing out each step you take to solve a problem will help solidify the process in your mind, and you'll be more likely to remember it during the test.

Modality

Modality simply refers to the means or method by which you study. Choosing a study modality that fits your own individual learning style is crucial. No two people learn best in exactly the same way, so it's important to know your strengths and use them to your advantage.

For example, if you learn best by visualization, focus on visualizing a concept in your mind and draw an image or a diagram. Try color-coding your notes, illustrating them, or creating symbols that will trigger your mind to recall a learned concept. If you learn best by hearing or discussing information, find a study partner who learns the same way or read aloud to yourself. Think about how to put the information in your own words. Imagine that you are giving a lecture on the topic and record yourself so you can listen to it later.

For any learning style, flashcards can be helpful. Organize the information so you can take advantage of spare moments to review. Underline key words or phrases. Use different colors for different categories. Mnemonic devices (such as creating a short list in which every item starts with the same letter) can also help with retention. Find what works best for you and use it to store the information in your mind most effectively and easily.

Secret Key #3 – Practice the Right Way

Your success on test day depends not only on how many hours you put into preparing, but also on whether you prepared the right way. It's good to check along the way to see if your studying is paying off. One of the most effective ways to do this is by taking practice tests to evaluate your progress. Practice tests are useful because they show exactly where you need to improve. Every time you take a practice test, pay special attention to these three groups of questions:

- The questions you got wrong
- The questions you had to guess on, even if you guessed right
- The questions you found difficult or slow to work through

This will show you exactly what your weak areas are, and where you need to devote more study time. Ask yourself why each of these questions gave you trouble. Was it because you didn't understand the material? Was it because you didn't remember the vocabulary? Do you need more repetitions on this type of question to build speed and confidence? Dig into those questions and figure out how you can strengthen your weak areas as you go back to review the material.

Additionally, many practice tests have a section explaining the answer choices. It can be tempting to read the explanation and think that you now have a good understanding of the concept. However, an explanation likely only covers part of the question's broader context. Even if the explanation makes perfect sense, **go back and investigate** every concept related to the question until you're positive you have a thorough understanding.

As you go along, keep in mind that the practice test is just that: practice. Memorizing these questions and answers will not be very helpful on the actual test because it is unlikely to have any of the same exact questions. If you only know the right answers to the sample questions, you won't be prepared for the real thing. **Study the concepts** until you understand them fully, and then you'll be able to answer any question that shows up on the test.

It's important to wait on the practice tests until you're ready. If you take a test on your first day of study, you may be overwhelmed by the amount of material covered and how much you need to learn. Work up to it gradually.

On test day, you'll need to be prepared for answering questions, managing your time, and using the test-taking strategies you've learned. It's a lot to balance, like a mental marathon that will have a big impact on your future. Like training for a marathon, you'll need to start slowly and work your way up. When test day arrives, you'll be ready.

Start with the strategies you've read in the first two Secret Keys—plan your course and study in the way that works best for you. If you have time, consider using multiple study resources to get different approaches to the same concepts. It can be helpful to see difficult concepts from more than one angle. Then find a good source for practice tests. Many times, the test website will suggest potential study resources or provide sample tests.

Practice Test Strategy

If you're able to find at least three practice tests, we recommend this strategy:

Untimed and Open-Book Practice

Take the first test with no time constraints and with your notes and study guide handy. Take your time and focus on applying the strategies you've learned.

Timed and Open-Book Practice

Take the second practice test open-book as well, but set a timer and practice pacing yourself to finish in time.

Timed and Closed-Book Practice

Take any other practice tests as if it were test day. Set a timer and put away your study materials. Sit at a table or desk in a quiet room, imagine yourself at the testing center, and answer questions as quickly and accurately as possible.

Keep repeating timed and closed-book tests on a regular basis until you run out of practice tests or it's time for the actual test. Your mind will be ready for the schedule and stress of test day, and you'll be able to focus on recalling the material you've learned.

Secret Key #4 – Pace Yourself

Once you're fully prepared for the material on the test, your biggest challenge on test day will be managing your time. Just knowing that the clock is ticking can make you panic even if you have plenty of time left. Work on pacing yourself so you can build confidence against the time constraints of the exam. Pacing is a difficult skill to master, especially in a high-pressure environment, so **practice is vital**.

Set time expectations for your pace based on how much time is available. For example, if a section has 60 questions and the time limit is 30 minutes, you know you have to average 30 seconds or less per question in order to answer them all. Although 30 seconds is the hard limit, set 25 seconds per question as your goal, so you reserve extra time to spend on harder questions. When you budget extra time for the harder questions, you no longer have any reason to stress when those questions take longer to answer.

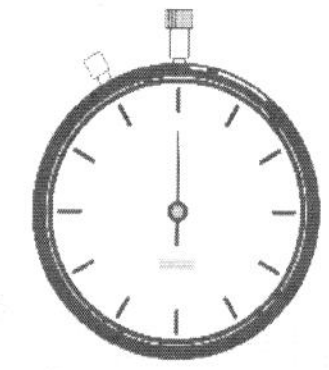

Don't let this time expectation distract you from working through the test at a calm, steady pace, but keep it in mind so you don't spend too much time on any one question. Recognize that taking extra time on one question you don't understand may keep you from answering two that you do understand later in the test. If your time limit for a question is up and you're still not sure of the answer, mark it and move on, and come back to it later if the time and the test format allow. If the testing format doesn't allow you to return to earlier questions, just make an educated guess; then put it out of your mind and move on.

On the easier questions, be careful not to rush. It may seem wise to hurry through them so you have more time for the challenging ones, but it's not worth missing one if you know the concept and just didn't take the time to read the question fully. Work efficiently but make sure you understand the question and have looked at all of the answer choices, since more than one may seem right at first.

Even if you're paying attention to the time, you may find yourself a little behind at some point. You should speed up to get back on track, but do so wisely. Don't panic; just take a few seconds less on each question until you're caught up. Don't guess without thinking, but do look through the answer choices and eliminate any you know are wrong. If you can get down to two choices, it is often worthwhile to guess from those. Once you've chosen an answer, move on and don't dwell on any that you skipped or had to hurry through. If a question was taking too long, chances are it was one of the harder ones, so you weren't as likely to get it right anyway.

On the other hand, if you find yourself getting ahead of schedule, it may be beneficial to slow down a little. The more quickly you work, the more likely you are to make a careless mistake that will affect your score. You've budgeted time for each question, so don't be afraid to spend that time. Practice an efficient but careful pace to get the most out of the time you have.

Secret Key #5 – Have a Plan for Guessing

When you're taking the test, you may find yourself stuck on a question. Some of the answer choices seem better than others, but you don't see the one answer choice that is obviously correct. What do you do?

The scenario described above is very common, yet most test takers have not effectively prepared for it. Developing and practicing a plan for guessing may be one of the single most effective uses of your time as you get ready for the exam.

In developing your plan for guessing, there are three questions to address:

- When should you start the guessing process?
- How should you narrow down the choices?
- Which answer should you choose?

When to Start the Guessing Process

Unless your plan for guessing is to select C every time (which, despite its merits, is not what we recommend), you need to leave yourself enough time to apply your answer elimination strategies. Since you have a limited amount of time for each question, that means that if you're going to give yourself the best shot at guessing correctly, you have to decide quickly whether or not you will guess.

Of course, the best-case scenario is that you don't have to guess at all, so first, see if you can answer the question based on your knowledge of the subject and basic reasoning skills. Focus on the key words in the question and try to jog your memory of related topics. Give yourself a chance to bring the knowledge to mind, but once you realize that you don't have (or you can't access) the knowledge you need to answer the question, it's time to start the guessing process.

It's almost always better to start the guessing process too early than too late. It only takes a few seconds to remember something and answer the question from knowledge. Carefully eliminating wrong answer choices takes longer. Plus, going through the process of eliminating answer choices can actually help jog your memory.

Summary: Start the guessing process as soon as you decide that you can't answer the question based on your knowledge.

How to Narrow Down the Choices

The next chapter in this book (**Test-Taking Strategies**) includes a wide range of strategies for how to approach questions and how to look for answer choices to eliminate. You will definitely want to read those carefully, practice them, and figure out which ones work best for you. Here though, we're going to address a mindset rather than a particular strategy.

Your odds of guessing an answer correctly depend on how many options you are choosing from.

Number of options left	5	4	3	2	1
Odds of guessing correctly	20%	25%	33%	50%	100%

You can see from this chart just how valuable it is to be able to eliminate incorrect answers and make an educated guess, but there are two things that many test takers do that cause them to miss out on the benefits of guessing:

- Accidentally eliminating the correct answer
- Selecting an answer based on an impression

We'll look at the first one here, and the second one in the next section.

To avoid accidentally eliminating the correct answer, we recommend a thought exercise called **the $5 challenge**. In this challenge, you only eliminate an answer choice from contention if you are willing to bet $5 on it being wrong. Why $5? Five dollars is a small but not insignificant amount of money. It's an amount you could afford to lose but wouldn't want to throw away. And while losing $5 once might not hurt too much, doing it twenty times will set you back $100. In the same way, each small decision you make—eliminating a choice here, guessing on a question there—won't by itself impact your score very much, but when you put them all together, they can make a big difference. By holding each answer choice elimination decision to a higher standard, you can reduce the risk of accidentally eliminating the correct answer.

The $5 challenge can also be applied in a positive sense: If you are willing to bet $5 that an answer choice *is* correct, go ahead and mark it as correct.

Summary: Only eliminate an answer choice if you are willing to bet $5 that it is wrong.

Which Answer to Choose

You're taking the test. You've run into a hard question and decided you'll have to guess. You've eliminated all the answer choices you're willing to bet $5 on. Now you have to pick an answer. Why do we even need to talk about this? Why can't you just pick whichever one you feel like when the time comes?

The answer to these questions is that if you don't come into the test with a plan, you'll rely on your impression to select an answer choice, and if you do that, you risk falling into a trap. The test writers know that everyone who takes their test will be guessing on some of the questions, so they intentionally write wrong answer choices to seem plausible. You still have to pick an answer though, and if the wrong answer choices are designed to look right, how can you ever be sure that you're not falling for their trap? The best solution we've found to this dilemma is to take the decision out of your hands entirely. Here is the process we recommend:

Once you've eliminated any choices that you are confident (willing to bet $5) are wrong, select the first remaining choice as your answer.

Whether you choose to select the first remaining choice, the second, or the last, the important thing is that you use some preselected standard. Using this approach guarantees that you will not be enticed into selecting an answer choice that looks right, because you are not basing your decision on how the answer choices look.

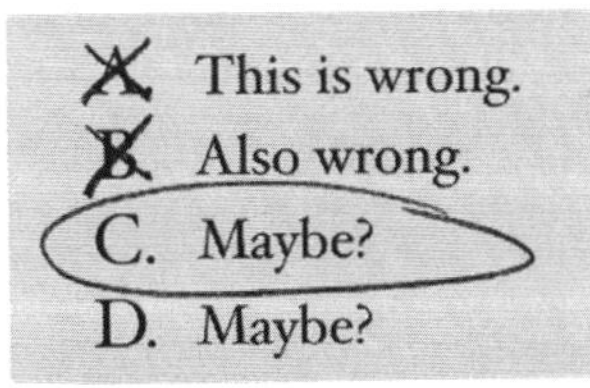

This is not meant to make you question your knowledge. Instead, it is to help you recognize the difference between your knowledge and your impressions. There's a huge difference between thinking an answer is right because of what you know, and thinking an answer is right because it looks or sounds like it should be right.

Summary: To ensure that your selection is appropriately random, make a predetermined selection from among all answer choices you have not eliminated.

Test-Taking Strategies

This section contains a list of test-taking strategies that you may find helpful as you work through the test. By taking what you know and applying logical thought, you can maximize your chances of answering any question correctly!

It is very important to realize that every question is different and every person is different: no single strategy will work on every question, and no single strategy will work for every person. That's why we've included all of them here, so you can try them out and determine which ones work best for different types of questions and which ones work best for you.

Question Strategies

✓ Read Carefully

Read the question and the answer choices carefully. Don't miss the question because you misread the terms. You have plenty of time to read each question thoroughly and make sure you understand what is being asked. Yet a happy medium must be attained, so don't waste too much time. You must read carefully and efficiently.

✓ Contextual Clues

Look for contextual clues. If the question includes a word you are not familiar with, look at the immediate context for some indication of what the word might mean. Contextual clues can often give you all the information you need to decipher the meaning of an unfamiliar word. Even if you can't determine the meaning, you may be able to narrow down the possibilities enough to make a solid guess at the answer to the question.

✓ Prefixes

If you're having trouble with a word in the question or answer choices, try dissecting it. Take advantage of every clue that the word might include. Prefixes can be a huge help. Usually, they allow you to determine a basic meaning. *Pre-* means before, *post-* means after, *pro-* is positive, *de-* is negative. From prefixes, you can get an idea of the general meaning of the word and try to put it into context.

✓ Hedge Words

Watch out for critical hedge words, such as *likely, may, can, often, almost, mostly, usually, generally, rarely,* and *sometimes.* Question writers insert these hedge phrases to cover every possibility. Often an answer choice will be wrong simply because it leaves no room for exception. Be on guard for answer choices that have definitive words such as *exactly* and *always.*

✓ Switchback Words

Stay alert for *switchbacks*. These are the words and phrases frequently used to alert you to shifts in thought. The most common switchback words are *but, although*, and *however*. Others include *nevertheless, on the other hand, even though, while, in spite of, despite*, and *regardless of.* Switchback words are important to catch because they can change the direction of the question or an answer choice.

✓ Face Value

When in doubt, use common sense. Accept the situation in the problem at face value. Don't read too much into it. These problems will not require you to make wild assumptions. If you have to go beyond creativity and warp time or space in order to have an answer choice fit the question, then you should move on and consider the other answer choices. These are normal problems rooted in reality. The applicable relationship or explanation may not be readily apparent, but it is there for you to figure out. Use your common sense to interpret anything that isn't clear.

Answer Choice Strategies

✓ Answer Selection

The most thorough way to pick an answer choice is to identify and eliminate wrong answers until only one is left, then confirm it is the correct answer. Sometimes an answer choice may immediately seem right, but be careful. The test writers will usually put more than one reasonable answer choice on each question, so take a second to read all of them and make sure that the other choices are not equally obvious. As long as you have time left, it is better to read every answer choice than to pick the first one that looks right without checking the others.

✓ Answer Choice Families

An answer choice family consists of two (in rare cases, three) answer choices that are very similar in construction and cannot all be true at the same time. If you see two answer choices that are direct opposites or parallels, one of them is usually the correct answer. For instance, if one answer choice says that quantity *x* increases and another either says that quantity *x* decreases (opposite) or says that quantity *y* increases (parallel), then those answer choices would fall into the same family. An answer choice that doesn't match the construction of the answer choice family is more likely to be incorrect. Most questions will not have answer choice families, but when they do appear, you should be prepared to recognize them.

✓ Eliminate Answers

Eliminate answer choices as soon as you realize they are wrong, but make sure you consider all possibilities. If you are eliminating answer choices and realize that the last one you are left with is also wrong, don't panic. Start over and consider each choice again. There may be something you missed the first time that you will realize on the second pass.

✓ Avoid Fact Traps

Don't be distracted by an answer choice that is factually true but doesn't answer the question. You are looking for the choice that answers the question. Stay focused on what the question is asking for so you don't accidentally pick an answer that is true but incorrect. Always go back to the question and make sure the answer choice you've selected actually answers the question and is not merely a true statement.

✓ Extreme Statements

In general, you should avoid answers that put forth extreme actions as standard practice or proclaim controversial ideas as established fact. An answer choice that states the "process should be used in certain situations, if..." is much more likely to be correct than one that states the "process should be discontinued completely." The first is a calm rational statement and doesn't even make a definitive, uncompromising stance, using a hedge word *if* to provide wiggle room, whereas the second choice is far more extreme.

☑ Benchmark

As you read through the answer choices and you come across one that seems to answer the question well, mentally select that answer choice. This is not your final answer, but it's the one that will help you evaluate the other answer choices. The one that you selected is your benchmark or standard for judging each of the other answer choices. Every other answer choice must be compared to your benchmark. That choice is correct until proven otherwise by another answer choice beating it. If you find a better answer, then that one becomes your new benchmark. Once you've decided that no other choice answers the question as well as your benchmark, you have your final answer.

☑ Predict the Answer

Before you even start looking at the answer choices, it is often best to try to predict the answer. When you come up with the answer on your own, it is easier to avoid distractions and traps because you will know exactly what to look for. The right answer choice is unlikely to be word-for-word what you came up with, but it should be a close match. Even if you are confident that you have the right answer, you should still take the time to read each option before moving on.

General Strategies

☑ Tough Questions

If you are stumped on a problem or it appears too hard or too difficult, don't waste time. Move on! Remember though, if you can quickly check for obviously incorrect answer choices, your chances of guessing correctly are greatly improved. Before you completely give up, at least try to knock out a couple of possible answers. Eliminate what you can and then guess at the remaining answer choices before moving on.

☑ Check Your Work

Since you will probably not know every term listed and the answer to every question, it is important that you get credit for the ones that you do know. Don't miss any questions through careless mistakes. If at all possible, try to take a second to look back over your answer selection and make sure you've selected the correct answer choice and haven't made a costly careless mistake (such as marking an answer choice that you didn't mean to mark). This quick double check should more than pay for itself in caught mistakes for the time it costs.

☑ Pace Yourself

It's easy to be overwhelmed when you're looking at a page full of questions; your mind is confused and full of random thoughts, and the clock is ticking down faster than you would like. Calm down and maintain the pace that you have set for yourself. Especially as you get down to the last few minutes of the test, don't let the small numbers on the clock make you panic. As long as you are on track by monitoring your pace, you are guaranteed to have time for each question.

☑ Don't Rush

It is very easy to make errors when you are in a hurry. Maintaining a fast pace in answering questions is pointless if it makes you miss questions that you would have gotten right otherwise. Test writers like to include distracting information and wrong answers that seem right. Taking a little extra time to avoid careless mistakes can make all the difference in your test score. Find a pace that allows you to be confident in the answers that you select.

⊘ Keep Moving

Panicking will not help you pass the test, so do your best to stay calm and keep moving. Taking deep breaths and going through the answer elimination steps you practiced can help to break through a stress barrier and keep your pace.

Final Notes

The combination of a solid foundation of content knowledge and the confidence that comes from practicing your plan for applying that knowledge is the key to maximizing your performance on test day. As your foundation of content knowledge is built up and strengthened, you'll find that the strategies included in this chapter become more and more effective in helping you quickly sift through the distractions and traps of the test to isolate the correct answer.

Now that you're preparing to move forward into the test content chapters of this book, be sure to keep your goal in mind. As you read, think about how you will be able to apply this information on the test. If you've already seen sample questions for the test and you have an idea of the question format and style, try to come up with questions of your own that you can answer based on what you're reading. This will give you valuable practice applying your knowledge in the same ways you can expect to on test day.

Good luck and good studying!

The Role and Kinds of Money

MONEY

A number of different ways exist to think about money, but perhaps the most basic way to understand money is as a commodity accepted as payment. When we say that something is a commodity, we mean it can be divided into smaller parts and transferred from one person to another. Kernels of corn, fishhooks, and coins all have these properties, and indeed all of these items have been used as money. In order to qualify as money, a commodity generally must be accepted as such. A commodity cannot qualify as money if no one will take it as payment. For this reason, even minted coins can lose their status as money. Likewise, a gift certificate for a certain store is not the same thing as money, because it is not generally accepted. Money is a commodity that can settle a debt or complete a transaction.

MEDIUM OF EXCHANGE

One of the functions of money is as a medium of exchange, or as a commodity accepted in exchange for goods and services. When you pay the cashier for a loaf of bread at the supermarket, you are using money as a medium of exchange. Societies without a monetary system are forced to barter, or exchange goods and services for one another. A bartering system can be more difficult to operate, since everyone must find a trading partner whose goods or services they want. When the society has money, people can receive payment in a commodity that they can then use in transactions with other people. The freedom afforded by money allows people to spend more time developing their economic interests.

UNIT OF ACCOUNT

One of the most significant qualities of money is that it can be used as a unit of account. As such, money fixes a clear value for goods and services so people can make comparisons and informed decisions. When one pair of jeans costs $20 and another pair costs $25, no confusion exists regarding which pair of jeans is more expensive. Moreover, the $20 pair of jeans has the exact same monetary value as four $5 pairs of socks. Without money, these sorts of comparisons would be impossible. When a society's money is stable and has an agreed-upon value, money is very useful as a unit of account.

REPOSITORY OF VALUE

Economists often say that money is a repository of value, which means money can be reserved for a time and then used to make purchases in the future. The money maintains its value even while being stored. Unlike perishable goods like plants or animals, money can be expected to maintain its value over time. Of course, in some economies rapid inflation reduces the money's value. However, for the most part, the American economy is stable enough to maintain money's value over a long period of time. A dollar bill buried in the backyard should still have approximately the same value if it is unearthed and spent in five years.

PHYSICAL PROPERTIES OF MONEY

In order to be useful, money must be portable, durable, divisible, and uniform. It has to be portable so it can be carried around and used as a medium of exchange. Extremely heavy coins or tokens would be useless in most economies. Money also needs to be durable, so it can retain its shape and appearance throughout a number of exchanges. If money can be easily spoiled or damaged, it will not be effective as a source of value. Money needs to be divisible so individuals can make purchases of different sizes. Virtually every type of currency comes in different denominations. Finally, money has to be uniform in order to be recognizable and accepted by the members of an economy. In order to be valid, money needs to retain a similar appearance over a long time.

Economic Properties of Money

In order to be viable, money must have a stable value, be scarce, and be acceptable in most situations. The value of money (that is, what a given amount of money is capable of purchasing) needs to be stable, although it is not necessary for it to remain the same forever. It is almost impossible to prevent minor amounts of inflation or deflation with regard to money, but a form of money that fluctuates wildly will be unpopular and unusable. Also, money should be somewhat scarce so it will retain its value. For instance, using blades of grass for money would not be possible because too many blades of grass exist, and more grass can always be created quickly. The demand for money must always be higher than the supply. Finally, in order to be valid, most parties in an economy must accept the money.

Commodity Money

Any form of money that receives value from the intrinsic worth of the material from which it is made is known as commodity money. The earliest forms of money—such as gold, jewels, salt, and rice—are all commodity monies. In order for these substances to be used as money, they must be scarce within the society useful to most of the members of the society. Commodity money made of precious minerals or metals must contain enough of the valuable substance to justify the money's face value. One problem with commodity money is that in times of extreme scarcity, people hoard coins rather than spend them. This hoarding puts a damper on economic activity.

Representative Money

Money that is intrinsically worthless but backed up by a valuable substance is called representative money. One example of representative money is paper bills tied to the federal government's gold holdings. In such a system, the amount of paper money cannot exceed the amount of gold held by the government. Systems of representative money were popular during the medieval period, when merchants and gold dealers would issue receipts promising to exchange specific amounts of gold for paper bills. Because representative money is tied directly to gold reserves, it is subject to fluctuations in value. Eventually, economists decided to move away from this system because they felt controlling inflation and deflation was impossible.

Fiat Money

Fiat money has no intrinsic value, and it is not directly tied to the reserves of the federal government. Essentially, fiat money acquires its value by direct order of the federal government. For this reason, fiat money is only valuable when members of the economy trust the word of the federal government. The United States uses fiat money, as indicated by the statement, "this note is legal tender for all debts, public and private" printed on dollar bills. The United States federal government in effect guarantees the bill's value, even though the money is not backed directly by gold or silver reserves. Using fiat money gives the federal government more control over the monetary supply, although some economists claim using fiat money leaves the currency vulnerable to inflation.

Money Used Today

Whereas earlier civilizations utilized useful or culturally valuable commodities like fishhooks or beads for money, most contemporary societies/countries use fiat money assigned value by decree of the government. Fiat money has no intrinsic value, since it is not made of valuable material. Fiat money exists in two forms: currency and bank deposits. Currency refers to all of the bills, notes, and coins that we use in economic exchange. Deposits refer to all of the money held in banks, credit unions, and other financial institutions, and can be used to make payments. A check is not considered money; instead, a check is an instruction for one bank to transfer money to another account. Similarly, the currency inside banks is not considered money, because it can fluctuate without changing the value of the deposits. For instance, when you withdraw money from an ATM, you simply are converting your deposit into hard currency. As a result, this action has no net effect on the supply of money.

Near Money

Very similar to money, near money can easily be converted into cash. Near money refers to any substance not typically used as a medium of exchange. Near money could refer to short-term government securities, Treasury bills, and time deposits. All of these assets are very liquid, but they cannot be used as a medium of exchange in normal transactions. In other words, one could not use a Treasury bill to purchase groceries, but it would be simple to redeem the Treasury bill for cash and use the cash to purchase the groceries. Because near money cannot be used as a medium of exchange, it is not included in M1.

Credit Cards

Economists do not consider credit cards to be money, since credit cards do not make payment at the point of sale. For example, if you use your credit card to buy a pair of shoes at the mall, you do not actually pay for the shoes when you swipe your card. Instead, you pay for the shoes when you pay your credit card bill a few weeks later. At the shoe store, basically you have obtained a loan from the bank that issued the credit card. The credit card, then, is really just a piece of identification ensuring that the proper account is charged for the value of the shoes. Payment is not made until later, however, so economists do not count credit card transactions as money transfers.

Electronic Checks

Electronic checks likely will become a more popular means of making purchases, especially online purchases. An electronic check is not considered money, because it merely instructs the bank to move currency to another account in order to complete a transaction. As such, an electronic check has no paper basis; although the early versions were designed resemble paper checks. The Financial Services Technology Consortium developed these prototypes. In the future, these checks will be sent and received through email. Many banks and financial institutions are excited about the advent of electronic checks, which they feel will reduce paperwork and lag time in transactions.

Debit Cards

A debit card functions much like a credit card, except that it draws from the cardholder's funds rather than from the bank's funds. When a debit card is used to complete a transaction, the bank receives instructions to transfer a certain amount of money from the cardholder's account to the recipient's account. As a result, the debit card functions just like a paper check. It is not considered money; instead, the debit card serves as a means of instructing a bank to move deposits. For most consumers, the advantage of a debit card is that it can complete transactions much more quickly than a paper check.

Electronic Cash

Governments, banks, and other financial institutions hope that electronic cash will become a viable method of payment in the future. However, in order for this to happen, electronic cash needs to be secure, convenient, and recognizable. Most designers envision a system in which cards are assigned certain amounts of money and then can be used to make purchases in stores. The difference between this model of electronic cash and a debit card is that the value of the electronic cash is in the card itself, rather than in the card's ability to move bank deposits. At present, the online company PayPal offers the most popular electronic cash venue.

M1, M2, and M3 Measures of Money

The composition of the money supply in a country can change quite a bit over time. For instance, in the past, hard currency accounted for a much larger portion of money than it does now, while the proportion of checkable deposits has gone up in recent years. Governments have two official measures of money, known as M1 and M2. M1 is the sum of all the currency held by businesses and individuals, all the traveler's checks, and all the checkable deposits held by businesses and individuals. M2 contains all of the funds included in M1, as well as savings deposits, small-time deposits, money market funds, and some other deposits. Obviously, M2 is much larger than M1. Finally, M3 is a classification of money that includes M2 as well as the long-term repurchase agreements held by banks and large-denomination time deposits.

Financial System

Finance consists of savings and investment. Money not immediately spent is either saved or invested. Savings refer all income and monetary holdings that are not spent. Investment, on the other hand, is money put to certain use in the hope of obtaining a future benefit. Investments can be either economic or personal. Economic investments are loans to businesses, while personal investments are the purchase of financial assets like mutual funds, stocks, and bonds. The financial system consists of the set of institutions that enable saving and investing. As such, this system includes bond markets, insurance markets, stock markets, and banks.

Commercial Banks and Other Financial Intermediaries

COMMERCIAL BANKS

Commercial banks are institutions with the authority to accept deposits and make loans. Commercial banks receive this authority either from the Comptroller of the Currency in the United States Treasury or from a state agency. At present, approximately 10,000 commercial banks exist in the United States. There are actually fewer commercial banks today than there were 10 years ago, because a trend of mergers has combined many formerly independent banks. Commercial banks accept checkable deposits, time deposits, and savings deposits. The highest interest rates are paid on time deposits, while the lowest interest rates are paid on checkable deposits. The interest rate on checkable deposits is often zero.

OPERATIONS

Ultimately, a commercial bank wants to increase its stockholders' long-term wealth as much as possible. A bank makes money by charging a higher interest rate for loans than it pays out for deposits. However, this policy presents some risk, because the chance that loans will not be repaid always exists. If unable to pay depositors wishing to withdraw their money, the bank will fail. While it is very uncommon for a bank to be unable to pay its depositors, in some situations depositors become very concerned and a large number of them seek to withdraw their money. This is called a run on the bank. In order to avoid runs, a bank must be especially prudent regarding the manner in which it makes loans.

CASH ASSETS

The assets of a commercial bank are divided into four parts: securities, loans, interbank loans, and cash assets. A commercial bank's cash assets consist of the combination of reserves and all the funds to be received from other banks as payments for checks. The reserves of a commercial bank include all of the currency in the vaults and the bank's balance on its reserve account at a Federal Reserve Bank. Commercial banks make deposits in a Federal Reserve Bank much the same way an individual or business makes a deposit at a commercial bank. In order to maintain operations, commercial banks are required to keep a minimum percentage of deposits as reserves. This safety precaution is intended to protect the bank from "coming up short" during large withdrawal periods. The percentage of deposits that must be held in reserve is called the required reserve ratio.

INTERBANK LOANS, SECURITIES, AND LOANS

Sometimes commercial banks have reserves in excess of the required reserve ratio. When this occurs, these banks are allowed to lend their excess reserves to other banks with a shortage of reserves. These interbank loans take place in the federal funds market. The Federal Reserve Bank sets the interest rate, also known as the federal funds rate, for these loans. Indeed, establishing the federal funds rate is considered the most important monetary policy enacted by the Fed. After cash assets and interbank loans, a bank's remaining assets are composed of securities and loans. Securities are bonds created either by the United States government or by another large, stable institution. Banks buy and sell these bonds depending on the interest rate. Finally, banks make money by loaning funds to businesses and individuals and assessing a high interest rate.

Advantages and Disadvantages of Saving in a Bank

One of the advantages of saving money in the bank is the low level of risk involved. The bank provides a stable interest rate, so there is very little market risk. Also, all deposits up to a certain amount are insured by the FDIC, so there is little risk of default. Conversely, investments in stocks and bonds are much more risky. On the other hand, savings placed in a bank do not have any protection from inflation. If the money's value decreases, the depositor has no way to recoup the loss. Also, the relatively low interest rate means that the investor will receive a lower long-term return on his or her investment.

National Banks

The United States government charters certain private banks as national banks. Specifically, these banks receive their charter from the Comptroller of Currency, a part of the United States Treasury Department. Law requires national banks to become members of the Federal Reserve System. Also, they are required to join the FDIC. Thus, national banks must maintain a certain amount of reserves with the central bank in their region in order to guarantee stability. National banks buy and sell government bonds, which helps to regulate the supply of money. Only about 30% of the commercial banks in the United States are national banks, although national banks are the most powerful banks in the country.

Comptroller of Currency

The Comptroller of the Currency (sometimes known as the OCC, or Office of the Comptroller of the Currency) is an agency of the United States Treasury responsible for chartering new banks as national banks. As national banks, these banks may be given surprise annual inspections, and they become subject to all federal regulations. Besides chartering national banks, the Comptroller of Currency also regulates services offered by banks, with the goal of promoting competition. The OCC also monitors the banking system in order to ensure that all citizens have access to services. The OCC investigates and enforces money laundering and financing of terrorist organizations involving commercial banks. Finally, the OCC oversees the conduct of national bank agents and affiliates, thus ensuring that these employees maintain the highest ethical standards.

Savings and Loan Associations

Savings and loan associations are thrift institutions that make personal, commercial, and home loans and accept checkable and savings deposits. Savings and loan associations have reserves, and like commercial banks, they are required to meet the minimum reserve ratios established by the Federal Reserve Bank. Most of the assets of savings and loans are held as home mortgage loans; for this reason, they sometimes are called building and loan associations. Savings and loan associations must register with the Federal Deposit Insurance Company (FDIC), which means that individual deposits up to $250,000 are guaranteed. In the 1980s, lax regulation led to a number of defaults by savings and loan associations, costing many depositors their entire savings. Since this debacle, the federal government has taken a much more aggressive stance towards savings and loan regulation.

Savings Banks

Savings banks are thrift institutions that primarily make consumer and home loans and accept savings deposits. In essence, the savings bank redistributes money from those persons who wish to spend less money than they make to those persons who wish to spend more money than they make. This arrangement enables borrowers to pursue the business projects that help fuel the economy. Sometimes the depositors actually own the savings banks, in which case the banks pay dividends rather than interest. Such institutions are called mutual savings banks. A savings bank holds reserves and must meet the minimum reserve ratio established by the Federal Reserve Bank.

Savings banks do not accept demand deposits, thus differentiating them from commercial banks. The general category of savings banks includes mutual savings banks, municipal savings banks, postal savings systems, credit unions, and savings and loan associations.

Credit Unions

A credit union is a thrift institution that mainly makes consumer loans and accepts savings deposits. Credit unions are owned either by an economic group, like the employees of a particular firm, or by some other social group, such as the employees of a particular state government. In essence, the members of a credit union loan money to one another. The interest rates are very low, in part because the loans usually are for small amounts. Most often, credit union loans are for medical emergencies, car payments, and household appliances. Credit unions hold reserves, and like commercial banks, credit unions are required to meet the minimum reserve ratios established by the Federal Reserve Bank.

FDIC

The Federal Deposit Insurance Corporation (FDIC) insures deposits up to $250,000. The deposits insured by the FDIC include retirement and savings accounts, among others. National banks are required to join the FDIC, but state banks are not required to join. The purpose of the FDIC is to promote depositor confidence and to prevent runs on banks. The FDIC occasionally buys or sells assets in order to enable a proposed bank merger. The organization was developed in 1933 as a response to the Great Depression. Member banks and thrift institutions pay for the operations of the FDIC. There are five members of the FDIC Board of Directors. The President of the United States selects the five members of the FDIC Board of Directors, and these appointments are confirmed by the Senate.

Holding Companies

Most commercial banks are run by holding companies, classified as corporations that own controlling shares of stock in a number of different businesses. A holding company can run many businesses without going to the trouble of merging or consolidating them. In addition, the holding company only has liability for the business to the extent of its ownership; since the holding company does not own the entire business, it is not solely liable. Holding companies enable banks to provide services not explicitly allowed by the Fed. These services include tax planning, investment advice, and data processing. Holding companies that administer a number of related businesses sometimes are referred to as parent companies.

Innovations in Federal Regulation of Depositary Institutions

Federal regulation of depositary institutions seeks to maintain efficiency, solvency, and liquidity, and most of all to reduce risks for consumers. Unfortunately, federal regulation does not always meet this goal. Accordingly, the financial crisis of 2008 illustrated the failures of the regulatory system. In the wake of these problems, the federal government has instituted a series of stress tests for major depositary institutions. A stress test is a computer model that measures a bank's performance after some cataclysmic event. In order to remain in business (that is, to avoid being closed or forced into merger by the federal government), banks must prove their durability and stability. At the same time, the government is said to be developing a systemic risk regulator that would measure the stability of the economy as a whole.

Restrictions on National Banks

The federal government places certain restrictions on national banks in exchange for those banks' rights to buy and sell government securities and the banks' respective memberships in the FDIC. National banks cannot lend more than 15% of their equity to one agent. Also, limitations exist regarding loans that national banks can make to their own directors and officers. As of 1999, national banks are allowed to engage in all financial activities with the explicit exceptions of real estate development, merchant banking, and insurance underwriting. It should be noted that designation as a national bank does not mean that the institution does business in all fifty states

Brokerage Companies and Insurance Companies

Brokerage companies are the primary depositories of investment accounts for the purpose of trading stocks and bonds. Formerly, brokerage firms appeared more distinct from banks than they are now. The main difference at present is outlined by the Glass-Steagall Act of 1933, which forbids banks from underwriting corporate securities. The Securities Investor Protection Corporation (SIPC) insures brokerage firms. Insurance companies are the primary vendors of life, health, property, and disability insurance. According to the McCarran-Ferguson Act, the federal government can regulate insurance if the state governments are not doing a good job. The National Association of Insurance Commissioners is composed of the commissioners of insurance from each state; this group has no power over insurance regulation but is charged with administering the law and recommending new laws.

Mutual Fund Companies

Mutual fund companies typically start open-end and closed-end mutual funds. The mutual fund companies then sell these funds to investors. The Federal Deposit Insurance Corporation insures these groups. The FDIC will reimburse a depositor for any losses up to the amount of $100,000, even if the depositor is not a US citizen or resident of the United States. The FDIC insures all types of deposits regularly received by a financial institution except for Treasury securities. Deposits made in different institutions are insured separately, as are deposits maintained in different categories of legal ownership. IRA and Keogh funds are insured separately from any nonretirement funds the individual may have at that same institution.

Regulation of Savings and Loans

In the 1970s and 1980s, the federal government limited the deposit interest rates that savings and loan associations could offer. This limitation created a problem when the interest rates rose dramatically, because customers rapidly withdrew their funds in order to invest in securities. This run caught many savings and loans by surprise, and in some cases institutional failure caused depositors to lose their investments. In the wake of this crisis, the federal government expanded the rights of commercial banks and insurance companies to include the services previously offered exclusively by savings and loans. At this point, the tarnished brand name made it better business for savings and loans to operate as components of other financial institutions. This arrangement remains to the present day; namely, to the extent that savings and loans still exist, they are called banks.

Deposit Institution Deregulation and Monetary Control Act of 1980

The Deposit Institution Deregulation and Monetary Control Act of 1980 was a counter to the trend of disintermediation. It established the Federal Deposit Insurance Corporation and declared that the interest rate ceiling would be eliminated within the next six years. Further, this act also gave the Fed the authority to set reserve requirements in order to ensure that banks would remain solvent. The act intended reserve requirements to remain between 3%and 10%. (This means that for every dollar deposited in a bank, the bank has to hold onto between three and ten cents.) The act allows banks to hold the reserve requirements as cash on hand, in a deposit account of the regional reserve bank, or as a combination of the two.

According to the Deposit Institution Deregulation and Monetary Control Act of 1980, the money in the vaults and the money held by the Fed does not earn interest. For this reason, banks typically hold secondary reserves in the form of securities, most commonly treasury bills. Primary reserves are usually held as cash, while secondary reserves are held as securities. This act gave the Fed more control over the monetary supply. When the reserve requirements go up, banks have less money to loan, and there is less money in circulation. This act also allowed savings and loans and credit unions to offer interest-bearing checking accounts, thereby putting them in direct competition with banks.

Garn-St. Germain Act of 1982

The Garn-St. Germain Act of 1982 permitted savings associations to offer their depositors money market deposit accounts with the same interest rates as the money market deposit accounts of the bank. This act also gave savings and loan associations the power to make commercial loans with a maximum value of 10% of assets. The act also allowed federal regulatory agencies to oversee and approve mergers and consolidations of troubled banks and thrift institutions. The Garn-St. Germain Act is one of the pieces of legislation credited with bringing on the savings and loan crisis of the 1980s, because it deregulated this industry and allowed thrift institutions to make risky loans.

FDIC Improvement Act of 1991

The Federal Deposit Insurance Corporation Improvement Act (FDICIA) of 1991 mandated risk-based insurance premiums. The point of the act was to safeguard consumers, who were justifiably wary of banks and thrift institutions after the savings and loan crisis of the late 1980s. One of this act's measures recapitalized the Bank Insurance Fund of the FDIC. The lower the capitalization of the insurance company, the higher the risk to depositors. Also, the FDICIA broadened the remedies available to bank customers. The act required the federal government to conduct annual inspections of banks and thrift institutions and to consolidate failed banks in the manner most beneficial to customers.

Federal Home Loan Bank system

The Federal Home Loan Bank system provides services to thrift banks. There are twelve banks in FHLB system. The eight thousand member institutions buy stock in the banks, and in exchange they receive low-interest funding and occasional dividends. The Federal Home Loan Bank is the largest provider of residential mortgages and funds for commercial development. The Federal Home Loan Bank Act of 1932 created this bank with the goal of increasing the volume of loans and mortgages offered by banks. Once the United States recovered from the Great Depression, the FHLB turned to community development and funding for low-cost housing.

Fannie Mae

The Federal National Mortgage Association, otherwise known as Fannie Mae, creates a secondary market for insured mortgages by buying and selling purchase commitments for them. This organization buys mortgages from banks. For the most part, this exchange is done to free up capital. The mortgages are used to create mortgage-backed securities that can be bought and sold. Fannie Mae itself holds a large portfolio of mortgage-backed securities. Fannie Mae was created in 1938 as a means of maintaining lending and bank flexibility. Also, it was hoped that the organization would make it possible for lower-income Americans to purchase homes. Fannie Mae issues securities on the New York Stock Exchange.

Ginnie Mae

The Government National Mortgage Association, otherwise known as Ginnie Mae, is the department of the federal government that guarantees high-risk mortgages. Banks and other financial institutions that hold a number of mortgages purchase pass-through securities from Ginnie Mae in order to maintain capital. These securities are called pass-through because they ignore all of the interest and principal payments made by the mortgage pools. Ginnie Mae does not issue mortgage-backed securities; instead, Ginnie Mae manages the market for these securities with the aim to promote liquidity and improve loan prices. The Government National Mortgage Association is a part of the Department of Housing and Urban Development.

Freddie Mac

The Federal Home Loan Mortgage Corporation, otherwise known as Freddie Mac, uses the global capital markets to provide support for low-cost mortgages. Freddie Mac originated as a way to help savings and loans associations sell their mortgages in tough economic times. It creates a secondary market in which traditional, relatively inexpensive mortgages can be bought and sold. Freddie Mac, in cooperation with the Federal National Mortgage Association (Fannie Mae), buys, sells, and guarantees home loans. The intention was to enable mortgage providers to offer more home loans, especially those they might otherwise see as too risky. Unfortunately, this plan backfired in the subprime mortgage fiasco of 2008, and subsequently the federal government took over Freddie Mac.

Disintermediation

Disintermediation occurs when depositors withdraw their funds to invest in financial instruments with a higher rate of return. Specifically, during disintermediation depositors take their money out of interest-bearing deposit accounts (for instance those maintained by banks and savings and loan associations) and use this money to purchase stocks, bonds, and money market mutual funds. Occasionally, restrictions on banks and thrift institutions make it impossible for these institutions to offer a rate of return comparable to investment vehicles. For instance, the skyrocketing inflation of the 1970s convinced many investors to withdraw their money from demand deposit accounts, since it was losing value quickly without accumulating much interest. When disintermediation increases dramatically, the federal government takes steps to level the playing field between banks and financial institutions.

Transaction deposits

The Federal Reserve defines transaction deposits as any bank deposits requiring the bank to maintain reserves at the central bank in order to back up exchange. The most common form of transaction deposit is the checking account. These deposits differ from time deposits, which cannot be accessed at any time. Transaction deposits are used to pay for other transfers of funds made by the depositor. Transaction deposits include demand deposits, auto transfer system accounts, and negotiable orders of withdrawal. Transaction deposits can operate in a number of ways. They may transfer money electronically, through share drafts, through negotiable orders of withdrawal, or through checks.

Demand deposits

Demand deposits are checking accounts that do not bear interest. Commercial banks hold demand deposits, and M1 includes these deposits. They can be withdrawn immediately at the behest of the depositor and without notice to the depository institution. Funds in a demand deposit account can be removed with checks, debit cards, check cards, or through electronic transactions. Demand deposits are distinct from time deposits, which cannot be withdrawn at any time. When a depositor writes a check from a demand deposit, the bank must pay the funds within thirty days. Demand deposits are included in M1, because the checks written from them can be used as a medium of exchange.

Automatic Transfer System Accounts

Automatic transfer system (ATS) accounts are deposit accounts that allow immediate transfer of funds from a savings account to a checking account. This enables a depositor to use funds in the savings account to pay for checks. Automatic transfer system accounts include both savings accounts that bear interest and checking accounts that do not bear interest. ATS accounts are included in M1. Further, ATS accounts are similar to negotiable orders of withdrawal. Most checking accounts issued in the United States at present are part of automatic transfer system accounts, since these accounts give customers the flexibility of a checking account and give banks the advantage of greater deposits.

Negotiable Order of Withdrawal Accounts

Negotiable order of withdrawal (NOW) accounts are checking deposits that bear interest. NOW account funds can be withdrawn on demand by checks, otherwise known as negotiable orders of withdrawal. Commercial banks, savings and loan associations, and mutual savings banks offer negotiable order of withdrawal (NOW) accounts. Mutual savings banks offered the first NOW accounts in the 1970s as a way to compete with commercial banks. Nonprofit organizations, some government departments, and private citizens are all allowed to hold these accounts. These accounts are popular because they allow the immediate withdrawal typical of a demand deposit with the investment of a savings account.

Automated Teller Machines

Automated teller machines are one of the most important advances in personal banking over the last two decades. In 2007, more than 1 ½ million ATMs were in operation around the world. An automated teller machine is linked to a central computer, which in turn has connections to the computers of specific banks. When an identification card is inserted into the machine, the account holder can check his or her balance, withdraw money, transfer money, make loan payments, and make deposits. ATMs have increased the convenience of personal banking, although some critics say that they encourage frequent withdrawals and irresponsible spending.

Acquisition of Financial Assets

When an individual or business decides to save money, the money goes to the agent of a financial institution. In return for the deposit, the agent issues a written confirmation, also known as a financial asset. This financial asset gives the individual or business the right to reclaim the property in the future. Some financial markets have been developed for the exchange of special financial assets like stock shares or corporate bonds. However, it is more common for a financial intermediary to facilitate transactions between savers and agents. A financial intermediary is any institution that receives funds and invests some of those funds in financial assets.

Financial Markets

Financial assets are purchased and sold in different markets. These markets are distinguished by the types of assets transacted, as well as by the length of the loan and the ability with which the asset can be resold. The capital market is the venue for the purchase and sale of long-term financial assets, while the money market is the venue for the purchase and sale of short-term financial assets. In the primary market, institutions can purchase newly created financial assets. Financial assets are resold in the secondary market. Financial markets exist as physical exchanges, as electronic venues, and as over-the-counter transactions. In order to trade some securities, individuals or businesses must be licensed.

Purpose

In general, financial markets are designed to raise funds. Governments, individuals, and businesses with surplus funds can loan these funds to organizations that need them to pursue projects or maintain daily operations. In return, the investors receive interest or a share in profits. One of the benefits of the financial market is as a spontaneous generator of money. When an individual borrows money from a bank and then invests it in the financial market, the money has a dual existence: it is an asset of the bank, because eventually it has to be repaid, and it can be used by businesses to make capital improvements. At the same time, financial markets keep money in circulation and prevent illiquidity crises.

Mutual Funds

Mutual funds are collections of money gathered from individual investors and managed by a particular company. The manager of a mutual fund buys a broad spectrum of financial assets and assigns shares to individual investors based on the amount of their deposit. Mutual funds are meant to be a stable investment, since the dispersing funds across a broad range of investments diminishes the risk associated with single stocks and bonds. For example, many pension funds invest in mutual funds. Most of the time, investors can reinvest their dividends to purchase additional shares of the mutual fund. If the net asset value of the shares increases, the investors receive capital gains. Net asset value is determined by dividing the total value of all holdings by the number of shares held by the investor.

Financial Intermediaries

Financial intermediaries act as liaisons between those persons or institutions with excess funds and those persons or institutions in need of funds. Banks are among the largest financial intermediaries. Credit unions, commercial banks, and savings and loans all act as financial intermediaries. Most of these institutions offer money market accounts and CDs, both of which are insured by the federal government. Banks make a profit on these transactions by lending some of the deposits to other borrowers. The banks then charge more interest to the borrowers than they pay to the savers. Obviously, a bank's ability to stay in business depends on borrowers paying back their loans in a timely fashion. However, past problems with bank solvency have motivated the government to establish a number of programs, including the Federal Deposit Insurance Corporation, to ensure deposits.

Not Associated with Banks

A number of the financial intermediaries that handle savings and investments for individuals and businesses are not banks. These institutions include mutual funds, pension funds, life insurance companies, and finance companies. A mutual fund collects money from individual investors and buys shares of a broad spectrum of stocks and bonds. A pension fund collects money and makes it available to depositors upon their retirement or termination from a given employer. A life insurance company collects funds that become available to depositors upon their death, disability, or attainment of a certain age. A finance company collects funds and reinvests them in businesses, typically to help maintain day-to-day operations.

Pension funds: Pension funds are among the financial intermediaries not associated with a bank. Employees contribute money to a pension fund so they will have some income when they retire. In many cases an employer contributes to the pension fund as well. For instance, some employers offer matching contributions when their employees invest in the pension fund. The pension fund manager purchases financial assets that offer solid growth with limited risk. Some distinctions exist among pension funds: open pension funds are available to anyone, while closed pension funds are only available to the employees of certain organizations. Public sector law regulates public pension funds, but private sector law regulates private pension funds.

Life insurance companies: Life insurance companies are among the financial intermediaries not associated with banks. Individuals can open life insurance accounts by contributing one lump sum or a series of payments over time. These funds become available upon the insured individual's death or disability. The insurance company invests the funds in financial assets such as stocks and bonds. Some insurance companies specialize in investing their deposits in real estate, although these companies are relatively few in number. Life insurance companies tend to invest their funds in safe securities, in accordance with their fiduciary responsibility to their customers.

Capital Markets

In order to qualify for a capital market, an asset must be held for a year or more. Capital markets are so named because the funds used to purchase these financial assets are often used to finance large-scale projects like the construction of new facilities or the purchase of large amounts of equipment. Some of the common assets sold on the capital market are stocks, bonds, long-range CDs, and mortgages. Investors in the capital market hope to receive a steady long-term yield. Businesses that sell securities on the capital market require some security, perhaps since they undertake long-term improvement programs that may not yield short-term benefits.

Money Markets

The financial assets traded in the money market have duration of less than one year. Because these loans are made for such a short period, they can only be used for day-to-day operations and small-scale projects. Some of the assets traded on the money market are short-term CDs, stocks, bonds, and Treasury bills. The Treasury bill market is considered the most secure money market. Indeed, Treasury bills are one of the only no-risk investments. Securities sold on the money market fund short-term expenditures, such as simply the funding the cost of continuing business operations. As a result, money market transactions are considered less secure in general than assets sold on the capital market.

Primary Markets

Financial asset markets can be distinguished by whether the assets can be resold. In a primary market, the financial assets cannot be resold; only the original buyer can only redeem them. Some of the financial assets traded on the primary market are small denomination CDs and savings bonds. The first issue of a stock, sometimes known as an initial public offering, also is sold in their primary market. In this case, investment bankers issue the stock to the public. There are three common ways to issue securities on a primary market: initial public offering (IPO), rights issue, and preferential issue. As previously stated, only the original holder can redeem financial assets sold on the primary market.

Secondary Markets

Financial asset markets are identified by whether the assets can be resold. Financial assets are resold in a secondary market. Liquidity, or the ability to buy and sell a given asset quickly, is one of the secondary market's investor benefits. This benefit gives investors flexibility, since they quickly can turn a financial asset into cash. The secondary market focuses on transactions involving stocks and bonds. The New York Stock Exchange is one example of a secondary market. The money market is another large secondary market. Further, in the United States there is a national secondary mortgage market. Securitization is the process of turning mortgages into assets traded on a secondary market.

Savings Bonds

Savings bonds are the only federal government security traded on the primary market. These bonds are made specifically for private, individual investors. Further, these bonds have proven very popular among investors looking to make a low-risk, long-term investment. The government issued its first savings bonds in the 1930s. The set of savings bonds known as Series E bonds helped generate funds for World War II. In recent years, the Treasury Department has moved to diminish the amount of savings bonds issued by the federal government. At present, savings bonds make up less than 3% of the public debt. Government savings bonds can be purchased online.

Stock Exchanges

A company first issues its stock in a primary market to investment bankers. This first step is an initial public offering, or IPO. This sale generates money for the corporation. However, following a stock's initial sale, it can be traded to other investors on a stock exchange. A stock exchange is simply a secondary market for transactions involving securities (stocks and bonds). The point of a stock exchange is to make trading easier by gathering all of the buyers and sellers of a particular asset. Private investors buy stocks in hopes that the stocks' value will increase so the investors can sell the stock at a profit. . All the profit made from the sale of securities is called capital gains.

Trading on the Stock Market

Investors purchase stock for a few different reasons. First, investors purchase stock in order to receive future dividend payments, or portions of the company's profits paid back to stockholders. An investor's dividend payment is proportional to the number of shares held by the investor. An investor may also seek to generate profits, known as capital gains, by selling the stock for a higher price than he or she purchased it. Some investors purchase stock intending to hold onto it for a long time; therefore, these investors do not care whether the stock price rises or falls—they are only interested in dividends. Other investors pay careful attention to minor fluctuations in the price of the stock, hoping to realize capital gains in the short term.

Common Stock

There are two kinds of stock, common stock and preferred stock. Common stock gives the shareholder more influence in the operations of the company. Common stock holders receive a share of the profits and also have voting rights. Nonetheless, common stock holders do not always receive dividends; the company may elect to reinvest profits in the business. Holders of preferred stock receive their dividends prior to common stock holders if the business is liquidated. Each share of common stock equals a single vote in the corporation. These votes decide the Board of Directors, which makes most of the important decisions about the corporation.

Preferred Stock

There are two kinds of stock, common stock and preferred stock. Preferred stock does not bestow any voting rights, but it guarantees dividends when the company makes a profit. Owners of preferred stock receive their dividends before owners of common stock in the event of a company's liquidation. Owners of preferred stock have no control over the corporation's Board of Directors, although individuals who own a large amount of preferred stock may be able to exert influence in other ways. Preferred stock offers less opportunity for appreciation (equity) than does common stock. Banks can only own a small amount of preferred stock, because it is seen as a somewhat risky investment.

New York Stock Exchange

The New York Stock Exchange is the preeminent securities exchange in the United States. It originated in 1792, and it has the highest dollar volume in the world. Over 1.5 billion shares are traded everyday on the New York Stock Exchange. Before 1996, specific stocks were located in different places on the trading floor. During the day, a representative from each stock held open bidding to match buyers and sellers. The price of a given stock would fluctuate rapidly in that system, but stock prices fluctuate even more rapidly now that traders use computers to buy and sell stock on the floor. At present, the New York Stock Exchange, the NASDAQ, and the American Stock Exchange all use a combination of floor trading and electronic trading.

Electronic Securities Markets

Many securities traders conduct their business outside of the traditional stock exchanges in deals called over-the-counter transactions. The National Association of Securities Dealers has developed a computer system that optimizes over-the-counter transactions. This computer system, known as the NASDAQ, has become one of the largest stock exchanges in the world. In addition, online trading has emerged in the last decade as a viable way for private individuals to trade around the clock and away from the traditional securities markets. Thus, online traders avoid some of the normal broker's fees and thereby improve their profit margins.

Money Market Funds

A money market fund is a financial institution that sells shares and uses the money from the sale to purchase assets. One of the most common assets purchased by a money market fund is US treasury bills. For shareholders, a money market account is similar to a bank deposit. However, in most cases, shareholders must keep a minimum deposit amount in the account at all times, and the size of check a depositor is allowed to write from a money market account may be restricted. Nonbank financial institutions manage money market funds. The value of these funds is included in the M2 definition of money.

Certificates of Deposit

A certificate of deposit (commonly known as a CD) is a pledge to pay the holder the amount of the deposit plus interest after a predetermined interval. The rate of interest for a certificate of deposit is fixed. Essentially, a certificate of deposit is a receipt from the bank. This receipt declares that a certain sum of money has been deposited and that it will repaid either at the request of the depositor or at a certain date. First introduced in the 1960s, certificates of deposit have become a common savings instrument. The most popular version is the time CD, in which the depositor cannot withdraw the large-denomination deposit without incurring a penalty.

Business Finance Companies

A business finance company purchases accounts receivable at a discount, thus allowing businesses to remain in operation or pursue long-term projects. Once the finance company purchases these accounts receivable, the finance company is responsible for collecting the payments. In some cases, a finance company also will purchase inventory and equipment from a struggling or illiquid business. Business finance companies also make loans at high rates of interest. Finance company profits are tied directly to interest rate fluctuations. The money required to run a business finance company is obtained from banks, thrift institutions, and money market accounts. For the most part, business finance companies can borrow at low market rates, in part because they experience such a low level of default. Public-owned business finance companies are often called money stocks.

Intermediaries Market

In the intermediaries market, sometimes known as indirect finance, commercial banks gather savings deposits and lend these funds to other customers. Participants in the intermediaries market include mutual funds, pension funds, insurance companies, and banks. The development of the intermediaries market has been a prime reason for the expansion of the global economy, simply because of the vast amounts of resources that had formerly lain dormant in bank deposits. Economists distinguish between direct and indirect intermediation as follows: transactions between lenders and borrowers (i.e., depositors and intermediaries) constitute direct intermediation, while transactions involving depositors, banks, and intermediaries constitute indirect intermediation. One general source of tension in the intermediaries market is that lenders prefer short-term arrangements (so they have ready access to their funds), while borrowers prefer long-term arrangements (so they can pursue long-term capital projects).

Prime Paper and Commercial Paper

Prime paper and commercial paper are short-term unsecured promissory notes that corporations sell at a discount. This sale offers a good way for businesses to raise money without dealing with banks. Commercial paper is a promissory note issued by a large business or institution. Commercial paper is unsecured and typically has a short maturity period, between 1 and 270 days. Commercial paper may be placed directly or by a dealer. The owner sells direct-placed commercial paper, while special professionals sell dealer-placed commercial paper. Commercial paper typically sells in denominations of $1 million and up. Prime paper is simply the highest-rated commercial paper and considered a responsible investment for institutions with fiduciary responsibility.

Debt Market

The debt market, otherwise known as the bond market, is the venue for the purchase and sale of debt securities, which may be either government-issued or corporate. Governments and corporations in need of liquid assets create and sell bonds that can be purchased by individuals and businesses looking to invest money with little risk. The money raised through the sale of securities on the debt market typically is used for long-term projects and major capital improvements. For the most part, debt securities are traded over-the-counter. Debt securities first are introduced in the primary market, and subsequent trades occur in the secondary market. . The debt market is several times the size of the stock market, although it receives much less press.

Equity Market

On the equity market, firms trade securities with ownership rights such as stocks. Companies sell shares in order to generate capital, and investors purchase shares with the hope of realizing a profit if the company performs well. The equity market includes both exchange trading and over-the-counter trading. Though the most famous component of the equity market is the stock market, there are equity markets in bonds, convertibles, options, and warrants. The most famous equity market is the New York Stock Exchange, although similar markets exist all over the world. In addition, many electronic markets for equity trading have emerged.

Treasury Bills, Treasury Notes, and Treasury Bonds

Treasury bills are short-term financial instruments sold at a discount. Purchasers derive profits equal to the difference between the purchase price and the face value. These bills are extremely liquid. Treasury bills have a maximum maturity period of one year. Treasury bonds are longer-term instruments; they mature at greater than five years, while normal bonds have a minimum maturity of only one year. The United States Treasury Department issues Treasury notes which have a maturity of between one and ten years. In other respects, they are identical to treasury bonds. Treasury notes have a fixed interest rate, and they pay interest twice a year.

Quantitative Analysis Performed by Financial Professionals

Modeling and simulation are two tools that financial professionals may use to analyze the possible effects of planned financial decisions. Probability analysis is used to determine the likelihood that a certain event will occur, often used to forecast the development of insurance rates and insurance risk. Financial planners often combine modeling and simulation with probability analysis in order to create a window into the possible performance of planned investments. Sensitivity analysis is a form of modeling in which financial planners consider how small changes in the market or in investment will affect the client's portfolio. An independent variable is adjusted to see how much change it will cause in the dependent variable.

Yield

Yield is the rate of return on a security. If the price of a bond falls, then the yield rises. The current yield is the rate of return or interest earned so far per dollar invested. Current yield, sometimes referred to as bond yield or dividend yield, can be calculated by dividing annual inflow by market price. Current yield is an estimate of the return an investor will get by holding a certain investment for a year. However, constant fluctuations in price affect actual yield. The holding period yield, on the other hand, is the rate of return or interest earned over the entire period the security is held, used when an investor expects to hold onto the security for an especially short or long interval.

Futures Markets

One of the smaller securities markets, the futures market, involves agreements to purchase or sell a stock at some specific point in the future at a specific price. An investor who purchases a future hopes that the stock's value will rise above the preset price, while the seller of the future is hoping that the value of the stock will be below the preset price. Futures markets have become popular in many large commodity markets because they give businesses some insurance against sudden changes in the price of raw materials. Some thriving futures markets are those related to cotton, wheat, and wool.

Options Markets

In the options market, traders buy and sell contracts that guarantee the opportunity to trade a stock at a future date and specific price. Unlike a future, an option does not have to be fulfilled. Typically, the purchaser of an option will pay a small percentage of the stock's current price in exchange for the opportunity to buy the stock at a preset price in the future. Options markets are extremely complicated, and therefore these markets are populated primarily by expert investors. An option to sell is known as a put option, while an option to buy is known as a call option. In the past few decades, the trade of options has expanded rapidly in securities markets, commodities markets, and money markets.

Stock Indexes

Even in a robust economy, the values of many stocks will drop. For this reason, discerning an overall pattern in the stock market without using a stock index, (a measure of a large group of stocks' performance) is difficult. The Dow Jones Industrial Average is the most famous stock index, although the NASDAQ composite and the Standard & Poor's 500 are also well known. At present, 30 stocks make up the Dow Jones Industrial Average. Stocks with a higher value weigh more heavily in the tabulation of the average.

BULL AND BEAR MARKETS

Financial professionals often use the expressions bull market and bear market to describe the climate for securities exchange. In a bull market, prices of stocks rise steadily over a long period of time. In a bear market, stock market prices decline over a long period of time. Because so much of the securities market rests on perceptions, a bear market's fear can contribute to a downturn in securities trading and damage to the economy. On the other hand, a bull market's optimism can spur robust trading that propels the economy.

SIPC

The Securities Investor Protection Corporation protects customers of broker-dealers as long as that broker-dealer is a member of the SIPC. If this member's registration with the Securities and Exchange Commission is terminated the membership in the SIPC also will be terminated. SIPC members/brokerage firms pay the cost of insurance. . If a brokerage firm fails, the customers get back those securities registered or in the process of being registered in their names. If the firm does not have enough funds in its customer accounts to satisfy these claims, the SIPC will pay the rest out of its reserve funds, up to $500,000 per customer. Commodity futures contracts, currency, and investment contracts are ineligible for SIPC protection.

NASD

The National Association of Security Dealers, Inc. (NASD) registers all of those people who sell stocks, bonds, tax-sheltered investments, options, mutual funds, and other securities. The NASD is an independent group supervised by the SEC. In order to register with the NASD, securities dealers complete a Uniform Application for Securities Industry Regulation, a Form U-4, and pass one or more exams. The NASD has designed a series of exams to test the competence of various financial professionals, from commodities traders to investment advisers. Once the individual passes the appropriate tests, he or she can become a Registered Representative and is licensed to sell certain securities.

REPORTING REQUIREMENTS FOR INVESTMENT ADVISERS

When an investment adviser registers with the SEC, he or she will fill out the two-part Form ADV. The first part asks for the applicant's background information and his or her expected clients; the second part asks for information about the planned fee structure, services offered, method of business operation, and the advisor's degree of involvement in securities transactions. This form typically restricts advisers from collecting fees based on investment performance, though the adviser still may base fees on a percentage of total holdings. According to the so-called "brochure rule," Registered Investment Advisers are required to submit a written disclosure to potential clients.

COMPLIANCE, STATE SECURITIES AND INSURANCE LAWS

The SEC asserts that financial advisers must keep detailed records. Any illegal actions committed by a planner constitute fraud. If an adviser fails to meet any of the requirements set forth by the Investment Advisors Act of 1940 or the process of registration, the SEC can investigate and confiscate all records. According to the Insider Trading and Securities Fraud Enforcement Act of 1988, investment advisers must keep detailed records in order to prove the absence of insider trading. As for state securities, investment advisers are encouraged to be aware of the "blue sky laws" in the state of their operation. Many states require a minimum capitalization amount in exchange for registration. States always regulate the insurance industry. . Advisers must register for each specific product they wish to sell.

Responsibilities of Central Banks

Central banks' primary tasks are to maintain economic stability, lend money to banks, and maintain reserves. Central banks supervise commercial banks and other financial institutions to make sure they are not making risky transactions. Central banks also control the supply of money in the economy in attempt to mitigate the fluctuations of the business cycle. Central banks do not loan money to individuals and private businesses, but they do make loans to commercial banks. These loans ensure commercial banks' ability to continue economic development. Finally, central banks maintain a large store of funds in reserve. These reserves guarantee the loans made by commercial banks and give the central bank control over the money supply.

Central Banking and the Federal Reserve System

Federal Reserve System

In 1908, the United States established a National Monetary Commission to investigate the country's monetary policy. This group recommended creating a federal banking system, and the Federal Reserve Act became law in 1913, despite some critics' claim that a central bank would place too much power in the hands of a small group. The Federal Reserve Act created the Federal Reserve System to provide an elastic supply of currency, helpful credit to commercial interests (and thus stimulate economic growth), and supervision for the nation's banks and financial institutions. After a long process of consultation with various business and government leaders, the Federal Reserve Bank as we know it today opened in 1914.

The Central Bank of the United States is known as the Federal Reserve System. The Federal Reserve System is like a bank for banks; it accepts deposits from commercial banks and other institutions and regulates the market. Individual citizens and businesses cannot make deposits with the Federal Reserve Bank. The Federal Reserve Bank is also responsible for conducting the monetary policy of the United States. Monetary policy is the regulation of the amount of money flowing through the American economy. Accordingly, the Federal Reserve System adjusts monetary policy in order to maintain employment, limit inflation, bolster economic growth, and minimize fluctuations in the business cycle. Although some economists contend that the market would be better off unregulated, most economists agree that the Federal Reserve serves a vital function.

Regional Federal Reserve Banks

The Federal Reserve System divides the United States into twelve regional Federal Reserve districts. A regional Federal Reserve Bank with nine directors administers each of these districts. The Board of Governors of the Federal Reserve Bank appoints three of these directors, and the commercial banks in each district elect the other six directors. . Each regional Federal Reserve Bank has a president appointed by the directors in that district. The Board of Governors must approve the president. . Regional Federal Reserve Banks are located in the following cities: San Francisco, Minneapolis, Chicago, Kansas City, Dallas, St. Louis, Cleveland, Atlanta, Richmond, Philadelphia, New York, and Boston. The Federal Reserve Bank in New York City is considered the most important of the regional banks, in part because of its proximity to the New York Stock Exchange.

FOMC

The Federal Open Market Committee (FOMC) is the primary maker of policy within the Fed. It has 12 members: the president of the Federal Reserve Bank of New York; four presidents of other regional Federal Reserve Banks; and the seven members of the Board of Governors. The regional Federal Reserve Bank presidents rotate out every year, so each region is represented equally and often. Every six weeks, the Federal Open Market Committee gathers and discusses the economy. On occasion, the committee decides upon some strategic actions undertaken by the Federal Reserve Bank of New York.

Chairman of the Board of Governors

The Chairperson of the Board of Governors is the most important member of the Federal Reserve System. The chairperson controls the agenda of the Board of Governors, as well as the agenda of the Federal Open Market Committee. In Federal Open Market Committee meetings, the person has the most influence over the proceedings. The chairperson constantly receives reports from economists and other experts, so he or she usually has the best information on a given problem. The chairperson also serves as a spokesperson for the Federal Reserve in meetings with Congress and the President, as well as in meetings with economic representatives from foreign countries.

Organization

The Federal Reserve System is the central bank in the United States, responsible for maintaining stable growth in the economy and creating monetary policy. The "Fed," as it is called, does not deal with individual accounts; rather, the "Fed" is the bank of private banks and other depository institutions. The Fed also regulates and supervises banks, distributes currency to the public through the banks, facilitates the collection and transfer of checks, and implements some of the regulations of consumer credit legislation. The Federal Reserve System consists of the Board of Governors, the Federal Open Market Committee, twelve Federal Reserve Banks around the country, various branches of these banks, advisory committees, and some member financial institutions.

Board of Governors

The seven-member Board of Governors is the highest authority in the Federal Reserve System. These members, usually renowned economists, receive appointment by the President, confirmation by the Senate, and serve terms of fourteen years. The board's main responsibility is creating and implementing monetary policy, although the board also must supervise the financial activity of banks, Reserve Banks, bank holding companies, and Federal Reserve System banks. The board decides how much money to loan these institutions and the rate of interest on these loans. Additionally, the board oversees any bank mergers and acquisitions for American banks, as well as those international member banks. The Board of Governors must report its activities to Congress.

Interstate Commerce Commission

The Interstate Commerce Act established the Interstate Commerce Commission (ICC) in 1887. At first, the commission only regulated interstate commerce occurring by rail or by a combination of water and rail. Now the commission regulates railroads, trucks, buses, water carriers, and all the pipelines not overseen by the Federal Energy Regulatory Commission. The ICC regulates rates that carriers charge and oversees any mergers, acquisitions, and sales of carriers. In addition to setting the rules for accounting, the ICC also grants the right to operate a railroad, trucking company, bus line, water carrier, or transportation broker. The ICC assures that the public receives fair rates and reasonable service guaranteed by the Interstate Commerce Act. Additionally, the ICC makes sure there is no discrimination, prejudice, or preferential treatment in the transportation industry.

Consumer Advisory Council

The Board of Governors of the Federal Reserve receives advice from three advisory committees. One of these committees, the Consumer Advisory Council, gives advice related to consumer protection laws. This group protects borrowers from exploitation by (CAC) financial institutions. Most of the Consumer Advisory Council's 30 members are representatives of the financial services industry and consumer protection groups. Group members serve three-year terms, and the terms of ten members expire each year in order to prevent drastic turnover within the council. The CAC has no real power except to lobby the Board of Governors. The Consumer Advisory Council was established in 1976.

Thrift Institutions Advisory Council

The Monetary Control Act of 1980 created the Thrift Institutions Advisory Council in order to serve as a liaison between the Board of Governors and thrift institutions such as savings and loan associations, credit unions, and savings banks. The Board of Governors appoints the twelve members of this council, typically representatives of thrift institutions. The members serve two-year terms and meet in person at least three times every year. The Thrift Institutions Advisory Council is not a statutory body, meaning that it has no authority to create laws or regulations. However, the group wields considerable power by directly lobbying the Board of Governors.

Federal Advisory Council

The Federal Advisory Council (FAC) acts as a liaison between commercial banks and the Board of Governors of the Federal Reserve. The FAC advises the Board of Governors on all matters pertaining to the Federal Reserve and can have considerable influence on the Fed's decisions. In particular, the FAC provides first-hand accounts of commercial bank operations so the Board of Governors can make informed decisions. The Federal Advisory Council has 12 members—one member from each of the Fed's districts. The representatives are commercial bankers, and each member serves three one-year terms. The members of the Federal Advisory Council gather at least four times every year, as mandated by the Federal Reserve Act.

Robert Morris and the Bank of North America

In 1781, Robert Morris led the creation of a charter for the Bank of North America. Modeled on the Bank of England, the Bank of North America was the first national bank of the United States. This bank was created as a reaction to the rapid devaluation of the Continental, the national currency of the time. Morris obtained large amounts of gold, silver, and bills of exchange, and issued currency backed by these holdings. Ultimately, the Bank of North America was too small to become a central bank, and several state banks successfully challenged it. Despite its problems and ultimate failure, the Bank of North America provided crucial financial resources during the latter stages of the Revolutionary War.

First Bank of the United States

The First Bank of the United States received its charter in 1791, primarily through the efforts of Alexander Hamilton. A proponent of a strong central government, Hamilton believed that a national bank would safeguard the fledgling nation's economy. The Constitution did not explicitly authorize the First Bank of the United States. Accordingly, many Anti-federalists, including James Madison and Thomas Jefferson, were concerned that a national bank would vest too much power in the federal government. Hamilton and other Federalists touted the value of a national currency. Although the First Bank of the United States took a while to gain footing, it eventually stabilized the American economy. Nonetheless, the First Bank of the United States died when its charter lapsed in 1811.

Second Bank of the United States

The Second Bank of the United States received its charter from Congress in 1816. Although the First Bank of the United States had been unpopular, the national government quickly realized that financing wars without a central bank would prove difficult. In addition, the absence of a national bank gave rise to all sorts of volatile currencies issued by state banks. More powerful than its predecessor, The Second Bank of the United States established a stable national currency. However, the Second Bank was not much more popular than the First, and Andrew Jackson eventually killed it in 1832.

Wildcat banking

In 1836, Andrew Jackson declined to renew the charter of the Second Bank of the United States and thus disbanded it. After this action, the federal government had no control of the banking industry. Every state bank issued a different paper currency and established different banking laws. Some states were extremely lax in opening accounts and making loans. Moreover, many banks purposely were located in faraway regions so depositors could not withdraw their money. These morally dubious institutions eventually were called wildcat banks and greatly damaged the American economy. Because they were so untrustworthy, these banks were subject to occasional runs, for which they often did not have sufficient reserves. The result was a period of occasional financial panic and general economic instability.

National Banking Act of 1863

After the disbanding of the Second Bank of the United States, the nation entered a prolonged period of economic instability. During the Civil War, the government finally issued a national currency. Government bonds backed these banknotes, and the banknotes became known as greenbacks because of the ink with which they were printed. The National Banking Act finally created a new set of national banks in 1863. This act created a new national currency and set requirements for national bank reserves. Furthermore, the National Banking Act levied district taxes on state banknotes issued after 1865, these taxes eventually led to the extinction of state banknotes.

Gold Standard in the US

Beginning in 1900, the United States government backed its currency with reserves of gold. In other words, each dollar bill issued by the government was equivalent to a specific amount of gold owned by the government. The government placed the economy on the gold standard in order to eliminate wild fluctuations in currency's value. Up to this point, the United States had suffered a financial panic roughly every twenty years. For the most part, the gold standard was successful in mitigating fluctuations in currency value. However, government economists eventually became frustrated with the limits imposed on monetary policy by the gold standard. At present, the United States holds much of its financial reserves as gold, but these gold reserves do not back the national currency.

Aldrich-Vreeland Act of 1908

The Aldrich Vreeland Act of 1908, a response to the Panic of 1907, established the National Monetary Commission, charged with researching foreign monetary systems and incorporating the findings into American banking reform. One of the eventual products of the National Monetary Commission was the Federal Reserve. The Aldrich-Vreeland Act also allowed national banks to issue currency backed by non-federal government securities and by commercial paper. Formerly, banks could issue only currency backed by government bonds. Banks could join in groups of at least ten and insure one another's deposits; this arrangement represented a sort of precursor to the FDIC. The aim of the Aldrich Vreeland Act was to increase the elasticity of the currency and prevent panics.

Federal Reserve Act of 1913

Even after switching to the gold standard, the American economy still experienced inflation and the occasional financial panic. Many members of Congress continue to believe that the economy needed a central authority to manage the money supply. Finally, Congress passed the Federal Reserve Act in 1913. This act established the Federal Reserve System, composed of twelve regional banks and a central administrative board. The Federal Reserve is essentially a bank for banks. As such, the Federal Reserve issues the national currency, makes loans to commercial banks and thrift institutions, and gives financial advice and services to other departments of the federal government.

Effects of the Great Depression on the Financial System

In 1929, the United States experienced the financial catastrophe known as the Great Depression. In large part, panic among depositors caused a massive run on the banks; many banks had insufficient funds and failed, hence causing the Great Depression. In 1933, Franklin Roosevelt led the passage of the Banking Act. This act established mandatory interest rates and prohibited risky bank transactions. Around the same time, the federal government created the Federal Deposit Insurance Corporation (FDIC), which guarantees bank deposits under a certain amount. These measures helped restore consumer confidence in the banks, although the United States did not rise fully from the economic doldrums initiated by the Great Depression until the Second World War.

Federal Reserve from 1940 to 1951

In the early 1940s, the Fed's primary motive was to support the war effort by keeping interest rates low by pegging. The lower interest rates and increased aggregate demand because of war needs increased the money supply, led to excessive money supply, and caused inflation. The Federal Reserve also pursued an aggressive policy of bond trading in the hopes of promoting liquidity despite fears related to the war. These policies were relatively successful; the inflation in this era was significantly less than that of the First World War. After the war, the Fed gradually released its tight hold on interest rates.

Federal Reserve-Treasury Accord of 1951

In 1951, the accord between the Federal Reserve and the Treasury eliminated pegging and kept interest rates from rising drastically. This Accord intended to monitor interest rates until they became stable. The Federal Reserve resisted this idea at first, because it meant giving up large portions of government-held securities. At the same time, the Treasury Department was apprehensive about giving up the pegging policy just as the Korean War was set to begin. The resulting agreement made the Fed the independent central bank it is today. The agreement made it unnecessary for the Fed to monetize Treasury debt at a fixed rate.

Fed from 1951 to 1970

From 1951 to 1970, the monetarist response to Keynes began to take hold among the directors of the Federal Reserve. One of the results of this philosophical change was an increasing emphasis on the money supply as the primary economic indicator. The Federal Reserve did not set specific goals or targets for the federal funds rate or interest rates; rather, it sought to stabilize the growth of the money supply. During this period the economy grew very slowly and inflation crept up. The Vietnam War began in the mid-1960s, and the Fed sought to expand the economy. A rapid increase in the money supply resulted in high inflation. Interest rates were lower, which raised aggregate demand and increased the money supply, resulting in inflation.

Fed's Policies during the 1970s

In the early 1970s, the Fed began to set intermediate targets, thus marking a transition from real bills or availability doctrines to quantity theory, the idea that manipulation of the monetary supply can and should stabilize prices and real GDP. One of the reasons for this change was the expansion of the money supply during the late 1960s, a trend blamed for steady inflation. The Fed spent much of its time redefining the money supply to include the new deposit forms offered by savings and loans and mutual savings banks. The confusion surrounding these transactions in part precipitated the financial deregulation that would spur the savings and loans crisis of the 1980s.

Stagflation of the Early 1970s

Stagflation exists when very little economic growth and rising inflation occur. During such periods, output stalls, and unemployment is high. In the 1970s, a dramatic rise in the price of foreign oil spurred inflation without an accompanying increase in demand and general economic expansion. Presented with a few options, the Fed could loosen monetary policy in order to create jobs and awaken the economy. This policy would increase inflation, but economists asserted that low interest rates would increase the money supply and spur development. The Fed's second option involved pursuing a tight monetary policy in order to restrict inflation. This policy would increase unemployment and would decrease the money supply by raising interest rates.

Fed's Response

Drastic increases in the price of foreign oil caused a corresponding increase in the prices of raw materials, which in turn led to persistent inflation. Unfortunately, an increase in the money supply did not accompany this inflation. Therefore, aggregate demand remained flat. In the late 1970s and early 1980s, the Fed increased the discount rate, set a marginal reserve ratio, and began setting targets on non-borrowed reserves. Unfortunately, the Organization of Petroleum Exporting Countries (OPEC) continued to raise prices, so the Fed's policies largely were ineffective. Unemployment continued to spiral out of control, thus forcing banks to raise interest rates, in some cases upwards of 20%.

Savings and Loan Crisis of the 1980s

For the most part, the history of banking since the Great Depression has been one of increasing regulation. However, in 1980 and 1982 a series of laws eliminated limits on savings interest rates. Savings and loan associations began to function like commercial banks, and many began to make risky loans. In some cases, these loans never were repaid, and the savings and loan associations failed. Many honest depositors lost their money in the savings and loan crisis. Reluctantly, Congress voted to help restructure the savings and loan industry, albeit at tremendous cost to the taxpayer.

Bank Mergers

In the 1980s, the federal government took many steps to deregulate banks. Perhaps most importantly, the federal government reduced restrictions on interstate banking, which enabled a number of small banks to merge. In particular, some large banks acquired small banks and used the existing infrastructure to enter new markets. In 1998, approximately 500 commercial banks were in existence, and in 2003, less than 200 commercial banks were in existence. Because of all these mergers, competition between the remaining banks has increased, thus creating more consumer services and low interest rates. Although fewer different commercial banks exist, more branches of each bank exist. Also, the remaining banks have larger funds with which to develop new technologies to aid consumers. However, some economists fear that the rise of enormous banks will diminish customer service in the long run.

Financial Services Modernization Act of 1999

In 1999, President Bill Clinton signed the Financial Services Modernization Act (also known as the Gramm-Leach-Bliley Act), which made it possible for investment companies, banks, and insurance companies to sell similar products in competition with one another. In other words, banks could now sell insurance, stocks, and bonds. Conversely, insurance companies and investment companies were now allowed to offer banking services. This act constituted a partial repealing of the Glass-Steagall Act of 1933. This legislation enabled consumers to complete all their financial transactions with one organization. However, each institution has suffered some growing pains while learning to perform the services of the other institutions.

Federal Funds Market

Commercial banks and other thrift institutions keep reserves at regional Federal Reserve banks in order to fulfill transactions and reserve requirements. These reserves, or federal funds, do not accumulate interest. Money constantly flows from banks whose reserves exceed the requirement to banks whose funds are less than the requirement. These exchanges occur on the federal funds market. The federal funds market evens out disparities in reserves, but it does not change the overall level of reserves. Funds acquired in this manner are available immediately. Most of the transactions in the federal funds market take place overnight, although some transactions, known as Term Fed Funds, are made for longer periods.

Effects of Changes in the Reserve Requirement Ratio

The reserve requirement ratio (also known as the fractional reserve requirement) is the percentage of total deposits a bank is required to keep in reserve. When raised, the reserve requirement mandates that banks retain more money, which means they can make fewer loans. Although the total amount of reserves stays the same, the overall money supply decreases because loaned money can be deposited elsewhere, thus multiplying its presence in the monetary system. The Fed usually raises the reserve requirement ratio in order to avoid inflation, which many economists believe is proportionate to expansion of the money supply. The Fed typically lowers the reserve requirement ratio in order to encourage lending and investment. Reducing the reserve requirement ratio has the effect of increasing the velocity of money and the money supply in general.

Effects of Changes in the Discount Rate

The discount rate is the rate of interest charged to banks that borrow funds from the Federal Reserve. Changes in the interest rates of banks and money markets follow changes in the discount rate. When the discount rate rises, in turn banks must charge a higher interest rate to customers. As a result, customers are less likely to seek loans, and the money supply is reduced. The money supply is reduced because money does not multiply itself in numerous deposits. On the other hand, a reduction of the discount rate encourages banks to borrow more money from the Fed and increase their lending by lowering their own interest rates. The net result is an expansion of the money supply.

Defensive Open Market Operations

The Fed undertakes defensive open market operations in order to counteract the effects of uncontrollable influences on the level of reserves. Tax collection is a classic example of a force that defensive open market operations must offset. When individuals and businesses pay their taxes in April, they are more likely to withdraw funds from commercial banks. The Fed anticipates this trend and buys securities to bolster reserve levels. Temporary repurchase agreements and timed repurchase agreements are among the most common tools for dealing with cyclical reserve changes. In some cases, the Fed makes repurchase agreements with an option to renew. This option means that the original deal can extend indefinitely at the Fed's behest. Finally, these deals give the Fed the ability to micromanage the money supply.

Repurchase Agreements

In a repurchase agreement, the Fed temporarily purchases securities with the understanding that the dealer will buy them back in the near future. These repurchase agreements temporarily increase the money supply and bank reserves. Often, repurchase agreements take place overnight, and the securities are repurchased on the next business day. These transactions have become a popular way for the Fed to make small adjustments to the money supply. Before arranging a repurchase agreement, the Fed typically declares the duration. The Fed makes these transactions at the discount rate and credits these transactions with federal funds.

Reverse Repurchase Agreements

In a reverse repurchase agreement, the Fed temporarily sells securities with the understanding that the dealer will sell them back to the Fed later. Reverse repurchase agreements diminish bank reserves and money supply, and can generate a small amount of short-term investment income. These transactions are secured because the government backs these securities. Additionally, securities dealers use reverse repurchase agreements in order to build up inventory and purchase other securities. In this case, temporarily owned securities serve as collateral to obtain longer-term securities.

Dynamic Open Market Operations

Dynamic open market operations are performed to tighten credit, ease credit, or increase or decrease reserves. Dynamic operations are not performed in advance of a predicted change, or in response to recent events. The Fed's ability to use dynamic operations has increased along with the rise of the monetarist philosophy among economists. Many economists believe that the Fed should concentrate on monitoring and adjusting the supply of money as a way of controlling inflation. Economists have paid more attention to regular, predictable changes in the money supply such as those changes that take place at the beginning of the week or month.

Fed's Supervisory Functions

The Fed has numerous supervisory functions. Specifically, the Fed distributes currency and manages transfers of funds between member banks. The Fed also issues and redeems federal debt. The Federal Reserve ensures that banks maintain reserve requirements so the banks will have sufficient liquidity to meet their customers' withdrawal demands. The Fed is responsible for processing payments and checks. In this capacity, the Fed acquires a great deal of information regarding economic activity and trends. The Fed is also responsible for researching the economy and staying abreast of changes that could influence the economy in general and the money supply in particular.

Announcement Effect

When federal regulatory agencies make an announcement or issue a report, the market reacts. This reaction is described as the announcement effect. For instance, the market rates typically move in the same direction that the Fed changes the discount rate. Also, the market responds to reports of a growth in the money supply, adjustment of other interest rates, and borrowing by the Treasury Department. The market perceives these announcements as heralding potential changes in credit and interest rates and seeks to adjust ahead of time. Sometimes, traders are aware that the Fed is about to make an announcement, but the traders have no advance knowledge of what the announcement's content. In such a situation, the market is especially volatile.

Credit Multiplier

The credit multiplier is a measure of the change in credit and in the money supply resulting from bank deposits. The credit multiplier is calculated as the change in credit divided by the monetary base. In the banking system, a deposit can more than triple itself in the form of deposits and credit. As an example, imagine a $50,000 deposit in a bank with a reserve requirement of 20%. The bank is required to keep $10,000 in reserve, but it loans out the other $40,000. The recipient of the loan deposits it in his bank, and that bank can then loan out $32,000 of the deposit to some other customer. The original deposit now is several times its original value. This is an example of the credit multiplier.

Required Reserve Ratios

The Federal Reserve's primary responsibility is to control the amount of money in the American economy. One of the ways the Fed accomplishes this task is by establishing minimum amounts (expressed as a percentage of deposits) for bank reserves. . In other words, every bank and thrift institution must keep a certain percentage of its deposits as reserves, in case there is a large withdrawal from the bank. Every type of deposit requires different required reserve ratios. The larger the deposit type, the larger the percentage each bank is required to keep in reserve.

Discount Rate

One of the ways the Federal Reserve regulates the amount of money in the American economy is by manipulating the discount rate. The Federal Reserve loans money to commercial banks that need funds to meet the required reserve ratio. The discount rate is the interest rate at which the Fed loans this money. In order to change the discount rate, one of the twelve regional Federal Reserve Banks to the Federal Open Market Committee initiates a proposal. If the Federal Open Market Committee approves the change, it passes the recommendation on to the Board of Governors. The Board of Governors makes the final decisions regarding changes in the discount rate.

Variations of the Discount Rate

The discount rate is the interest rate charged when member banks borrow money from the Fed through the discount window. The base rate is a benchmark against which adjustable rates are made. Sometimes, banks will give a base rate but indicate the possibility of a future adjustment within certain parameters. The repo rate, otherwise known as the official bank rate, is the discount rate the Bank of England uses in its loans to commercial banks in the United Kingdom and United States. The repo rate typically resembles the discount rate in the United States. The prime rate is the best rate of interest offered by a commercial bank; it directly ties to fluctuations in the discount rate.

Discount Window Programs

The Fed uses the discount window to extend seasonal credit, exceptional circumstances credit, and 14-day adjustment credit. When banks borrow at the discount window, they receive the discount rate. Banks typically borrow money at the discount window when they want to avoid problems with liquidity. In addition, the discount window is able to insure financial market stability by offering a permanent venue for financial transactions. At one time, the discount window was only available when banks already had exhausted other sources of funds. Gradually, however, the Fed has relaxed the restrictions on transactions made at the discount window and has traded with banks at any time as long as the banks can prove financial stability.

Open Market Operations

One of the ways that the Federal Reserve System adjusts the amount of money in the American economy is by buying and selling government securities, a process known as open market operations. The Fed sells government securities, including United States Treasury bills and bonds, to banks and private interests. When the Federal Reserve sells government securities, it reduces the amount of money in the American economy. When the Federal Reserve buys back government securities, it increases the amount of money in the American economy. The Federal Reserve does not sell government securities to other federal government organizations.

Monetary Base

The Federal Reserve is responsible for maintaining a solid foundation of money for the American economy. The supply of money maintained by the Fed, called the monetary base, consists of all the coins, bank reserves, and Federal Reserve notes held by the Fed. If the monetary base is large, it can support a large amount of money in the economy. All of the Federal Reserve notes and bank reserves held by the Fed are liabilities, since they are owed to other institutions. The Fed's assets include loans made to banks, government securities, and gold and other deposits made with other central banks. While the United States economy still is based partly upon gold, American currency is not directly tied to the amount of gold held by the federal government. The Federal Reserve also makes deposits in other strong central banks around the world.

Open Market Operations

Open market operations are the primary policy tool used by the Federal Reserve to adjust the amount of money in circulation. The Federal Reserve buys securities with money and with the creation of new bank reserves. The purchase of securities by the Federal Reserve decreases the federal funds rate, because the presence of more reserves in the banking system increases the number of interbank loans and decreases along with demand for interbank loans. The opposite occurs when the Federal Reserve sells securities. Banks and other institutions purchase securities with money and bank reserves. The sale of securities by the Fed diminishes the reserves in the banking system and decreases the supply of interbank loans. This in turn increases the demand for interbank loans and raises the federal funds rate. Typically, the Fed has a particular federal funds rate target in mind when it begins open market operations.

Effects on Lending

Open market operations (that is, the buying and selling of government securities by the Fed) directly influence the amount of lending by commercial banks and thrift institutions. When the Federal Reserve purchases securities from banks, it increases the reserves in those banks, thus enabling them to lend more. When banks lend money, they in effect create new money through the collection of interest. However, when the Federal Reserve sells government securities to commercial banks and thrift institutions, it diminishes the bank reserves and therefore diminishes the amount of lending done by banks. This means that less money will be created by interest payments from loans.

Multiplier Effect

When the Federal Reserve purchases securities from commercial banks and thrift institutions, it is in effect increasing the monetary base. This makes sense, since the money used to purchase the securities goes into the bank reserves, which then can be lent to individuals and businesses. Some of the loaned money will make purchases, buy new equipment, and continue business operations. However, some of the loaned money will be invested back in the bank. At this point, the money will exist in the banking system twice: both as an outstanding loan that the bank considers an asset, and as a bank deposit which the bank can use to make investments of its own. This phenomenon is known as the multiplier effect.

Check Clearing Service of the Fed

The Federal Reserve offers check-clearing services to banks, in which it records all the receipts and expenditures of the bank clients. The high volume of checks in each Federal Reserve District makes this a substantial undertaking, but the Federal Reserve speeds financial transactions and guarantee payment for banks. Unlike commercial banks, the Fed never has to worry about being unable to cover transactions. Because the Fed is in charge of printing the money, it has no liquidity problems. This generates confidence in banking transactions. However, in recent years, private companies have begun to take over check clearing services, and the Federal Reserve's role in this task has diminished.

Regulation of Bank Holding Companies and the Bank Exams

The Federal Reserve is responsible for supervising the activities of bank holding companies, institutions that own a controlling interest in more than one bank. As part of this supervision, the Federal Reserve administers bank exams that require the banks to supply detailed information on their accounts and practices. In particular, the Federal Reserve wants to assure banks are not involved in risky lending practices. Trained bank regulators review the institution's assets and liabilities and pay particular attention to the soundness of the bank's investments and the adherence to law. The Federal Reserve also wants to maintain competition among banks and protect borrowers from predatory loans.

Creation of Currency

One of the main tasks of the Federal Reserve is to create the paper and metal currency used in economic transactions. Only one official currency circulates in the United States, the fiat money produced by the Federal Reserve. The Bureau of Engraving and Printing, a part of the Department of the Treasury, prints the Federal Reserve notes and sends the notes to the district banks. Then the district banks lend to commercial institutions. From there, currency makes its way to individuals and businesses. The currency produced by the United States Federal Reserve lasts approximately three years, although larger denomination bills tend to be exchanged less and thus have a longer lifespan. The US Mint produces the coins used in the United States.

Monetary Transmission Process

The monetary transmission process is the response of the product, financial, and labor markets to actions of monetary policy. For example, when the Fed sells securities, bank reserves and thus the money supply decrease, interest rates rise, and investors buy securities. These actions deplete the money supply further and decrease aggregate demand. On the other hand, when the Fed buys securities the money supply and bank reserves increase, so interest rates decline. When interest rates decline, investors are less likely to purchase securities of their own, so the money supply will remain high. This abundance of cash in the system is likely to increase aggregate demand. An increase in aggregate demand is good news for retailers, among other vendors.

Recognition Lags Associated with Fed Policies

The goals of the Fed are to limit inflation, minimize unemployment, maintain a strong real GDP, and maintain stable prices in the financial and international markets. However, the Fed's ability to make accurate and timely adjustments to the monetary supply is hampered by recognition, response, and implementation lags. A recognition lag is the delay between an economic shock and the government and economic experts' observation of the shock. The duration of a recognition lag depends on the severity of the event. Events that may have a recognition lag include recessions and depressions, because these problems require assembly of economic data prior to their diagnosis.

Response Lags Associated with Fed Policies

The actions taken by the Fed rely on imperfect information and uncertain predictions regarding future economic events. The response lag, the delay between a policy's implementation effect, is one of the problems associated with action by the Fed. Most of the Fed's actions do not yield immediate results. For instance, if the Fed sells securities, the diminution of the money supply does not instantaneously lower interest rates. Economists estimate that the economy can take six months to respond to changes in the federal funds rate. To an extent, the Fed can consider the response lag when implementing policies. However, the duration of the lag is unpredictable.

Implementation Lags Associated with Fed Policies

Unfortunately, the Federal Reserve does not have the luxury of perfect information and immediate implementation. When a large macroeconomic event occurs, a significant gap, known as the implementation lag, emerges between the event and the implementation of a response policy. The implementation lag is longer than the recognition lag but shorter than the response lag. The Fed attempts to minimize the implementation lag by meeting regularly and giving the Board of Governors authority to call meetings at a moment's notice. Nevertheless, important decisions take time, and the delay between recognition and implementation invariably affects the utility of the Fed's policies.

Operating and Intermediate Targets Used by the Fed

Operating targets are short-term goals. For instance, in 1994, the Fed began setting a daily target for the federal funds rate. On the other hand, the Fed intends intermediate targets, as steps toward a larger goal. For instance, the Fed set intermediate targets for monetary aggregates, nominal GDP, exchange rates, and interest rates. The Fed does not set intermediate targets for the federal funds rate; rather, it seeks to control this rate through managing the money supply. In setting intermediate targets, the Fed monitors debt level, net borrowed reserves, total reserves, total federal funds trading, and other economic indicators.

Basic Demand Curve

According to the law of demand, higher prices reduce the demand for an item, while lower prices increase demand for an item. As the price of a product increases, consumers can find more substitutes or products that fill a similar role. In this line, consumers will respond more favorably to price when faced with more available viable substitutions. A demand curve, then, slopes down and to the right. Price elasticity is shown when a small change in price results in a large change in sales. When perfect elasticity exists, the demand curve is exactly horizontal. Price inelasticity, on the other hand, exists when a large price change produces only a small change in sales. A vertical demand curve indicates perfect price inelasticity.

Supply Curve and Income Elasticity

The law of supply states that a higher price increases the supply of a good. A supply curve is elastic when a price change leads to a great change in the quantity supplied. Conversely, a curve is inelastic when a price change produces only a small change in supply. The change in quantity supplied is simply movement along the supply curve. Factors that can cause movement along the supply curve include changes in resource prices, changes in technology, natural disasters, or other disruptive events. Income elasticity is the sensitivity of demand to changes in consumer income. An inferior good will have negative income elasticity, meaning that as income increases, the quantity demanded will decrease. Conversely, a normal good will have positive income elasticity.

Supply of Money

For the short-run, unanticipated increases in the money supply tend to increase aggregate demand. However, anticipated increases exert negligible impact on aggregate demand or interest rates. Few definitions exist for the money supply. M1 is the simplest definition, and this term includes currency in circulation, checkable deposits, and traveler's checks. M2 offers a broader picture and includes everything in M1 along with savings deposits, time deposits less than $100,000, and money market mutual fund shares. When money leaves the system, interest rates rise and drive down stock values (since the required rate of return increases and the firm's earnings will likely decrease).

Popular Economic Indicators

Investors whose livelihood depends on knowing the relationship between security prices and economic activity necessarily desire to hypothesize accurately the direction of economic activity. The ten leading economic indicators (as compiled by the National Bureau of Economic Research) are as follows: stock prices; average weekly work hours; average unemployment claims; manufacturer's new consumer goods orders; manufacturers' new orders for nondefense capital goods; vendor performance; new building permits; the difference in interest rates for ten-year Treasury bonds and the federal funds rate); inflation-adjusted M2; and consumer expectations from the University of Michigan Research Center.

Business Cycles

A business cycle is a pattern of changing economic output and growth. An increased rate of inflation generally accompanies the peak of a business cycle. When this increased rate of inflation occurs, unemployment rises and national output declines. These circumstances ultimately create a recession. The term recession refers to a period in which Real GDP declines for two or more consecutive quarters; a depression is simply a severe recession. The most common means of measuring economic activity is gross domestic product (GDP), the total value of all final goods and services newly produced within a country by domestic factors of production. Most of the time, economists use Real GDP (GDP adjusted to exclude the impact of inflation) and the unemployment rate determine the phase of the business cycle.

Law of Diminishing Marginal Utility

A demand curve slopes downward because the marginal advantage of using each good or service decreases with the acquisition of each additional good or service. This occurrence is known as the law of diminishing marginal utility. In this case, utility can include value, function, enjoyment, or any other positive quality obtained from a good or service. For example, if you purchase a car, you will get a certain amount of use and pleasure from it. If you purchase another car, however, even though you will obtain use and pleasure, you will probably obtain less satisfaction since you already have a car. This trend holds true for all goods and services and represents one reason for the downward slope of the demand curve. Since they intuitively know that they will get less utility from their fifth sandwich than from their first, most people tend to limit their purchases.

Substitution Effect and Income Effect

When priced lower, the demand for the same goods and services is higher. Two general explanations, known as the substitution effect and the income effect, explain this phenomenon. The substitution effect is the tendency of consumers to buy alternative products when the price for a given product increases. For instance, if the price of apples rises dramatically, consumers may choose to purchase pears at a relatively cheaper price. The income effect is the tendency to buy more when individual purchasing power seems greater. In other words, when a person perceives that his or her money is worth more, he or she consequently will buy more. If a pair of shoes costs $25 instead of $50, for example, the consumer will realize that he or she still has $25 left over and will be more likely to buy another pair of shoes.

Influences on Demand

Income, Complementary Goods, and Substitute Goods

The demand for specific goods in the marketplace constantly shifts. However, events that increase demand for some goods may decrease demand for others. For instance, when a person's income increases, his demand for luxury goods will increase, while his demand for inferior goods will decrease. Complementary goods, or products used in conjunction with other products, can also influence demand. Therefore, for instance, if the demand for peanut butter increases, the demand for jelly likely will increase. Substitute goods, on the other hand, are products that can be used instead of a given product. The demand for a product is inversely proportional to the demand for substitute goods.

Tastes, Expectations, and Market Size

Changes in consumer tastes can influence demand—for instance, when a once "faddish" purchase suddenly loses its "coolness." Businesses spend huge amounts of money on advertising in order to manipulate consumer's tastes for an increase demand for their products. Consumer expectations of price changes also influence demand. If consumers expect the price of a good or service to decline in the future, they will wait to purchase it. The size of the market for a product also influences demand. It seems obvious, but if more people are in the market for a given product, the demand for that product will be greater. The demand for a shoe for people with fallen arches will never be the same as for a regular shoe, since the number of people with fallen arches is so much smaller than the number of people without fallen arches.

INFLUENCE ON ELASTICITY OF DEMAND

Elasticity of demand partly depends on the ease with which consumers can acquire substitute goods. For instance, if the price for name-brand sneakers skyrockets, consumers easily can acquire cheaper generic shoes. The percentage of income spent on a given good or service also affects elasticity of demand. The demand for things that represent large portions of income tend to be more elastic; if the price of these expensive products increases, demand will decrease drastically. However, the demand for inexpensive items tends to be more inelastic, since a slight variation makes very little difference to overall financial status. Finally, demand for essential goods (e.g., food) tends to be inelastic, since people generally purchase these goods regardless of cost, while demand for luxury goods (e.g., silk sheets) is very elastic.

MARGINAL PRODUCT AND SPECIALIZATION

A business has to determine the number of employees that produce the most output per worker. The amount of output produced by adding one more worker is called marginal product. For instance, a sweatshirt manufacturer employs five workers and produces 300 shirts a day. If the company adds another worker, it will produce 380 sweatshirts every day. The marginal product of adding the sixth employee is 80 sweatshirts. If the company adds another employee, it will be possible to produce 480 sweatshirts, a marginal product of 100. The marginal product might increase in a scenario like this because adding new employees allows other employees to specialize on certain tasks. In general, employees are more productive when they can concentrate on a smaller number of responsibilities.

PRINCIPLE OF INCREASING AND DIMINISHING RETURNS

One of the struggles most companies face is determining the number of employees that will produce the most output per employee. When the marginal product of adding employees is increasing, it makes sense to continue adding new employees. At this point, the business is experiencing increasing returns on the addition of new employees. However, eventually, the marginal product of adding employees will begin to decline, perhaps because there will not be enough work to occupy all of the employees or because they are getting in one another's way. When the marginal product of adding new employees decreases, the business is receiving diminishing returns on its investment. The overall output continues to grow, but at a smaller rate, and the company now has to pay the salaries of a number of new employees.

FIXED COSTS, VARIABLE COSTS, MARGINAL COSTS, AND TOTAL COSTS

Businesses incur a number of different costs in pursuit of their ends. Fixed costs remain the same regardless of output. The cost of lighting a factory, for instance, is the same even if the factory never manufactures product. Variable costs, on the other hand, are dependent on the amount of output. The cost of raw materials, for instance, will be higher when the factory produces more products. The total cost equals the sum of the fixed and variable costs. Economists define marginal cost as the additional expense incurred by producing one more unit. In general, marginal cost decreases as output increases, although scenarios exist in which production exceeds capacity, and marginal cost begins to decrease.

MARGINAL REVENUE AND TOTAL REVENUE

Economists make a distinction between marginal revenue, the money earned from the sale of each additional unit, and total revenue, the entirety of money earned from the sale of a product. If a product has a consistent price no matter the volume sold, then the marginal revenue is constant. For example, if apples always cost 25 cents, then the marginal revenue of each apple sold is 25 cents. If apples are sold "3 for the price of 2," then the marginal revenue of the third apple is zero. Total revenue is calculated by multiplying price and quantity. In general, businesses try to find the point at which marginal cost and marginal revenue are the same. At this point, the ratio of revenue to cost is the greatest; therefore, profit is greatest.

INFLUENCES ON SUPPLY

INPUT COSTS, TECHNOLOGY, AND PRODUCTIVITY

A number of factors influence the supply of a good or service, but perhaps the most notable factor is the input costs of production. Input costs refer to the price of the resources required to produce one unit of a good or service. Input costs include labor, raw materials, and overhead. When input costs are high, supply tends to be low. Technology also influences supply: improvements in automation and electronic manufacturing can improve output dramatically without a correspondingly large increase in input costs. Finally, the productivity of the labor force influences. In economics, productivity refers to the amount of goods or services one employee can generate in a particular interval. Specialization and effective training increases employee productivity and therefore influences supply.

GOVERNMENT INTERVENTION, QUANTITY OF PRODUCERS, AND PRODUCER EXPECTATIONS

Certain government actions such as taxes and regulations can exert direct influence upon supply.. In particular, the government levies excise taxes on the production and sale of certain goods and services. Conversely, government subsidies are payments to the producers of a certain good or service. The government issues subsidies for industries, like farms, that it wishes to support. The number of producers also affects supply: an increase in producers will likely co-occur with an increase in supply. On the other hand, when only a few companies make a given good or service, the supply likely will be low. Finally, producer expectation can influence supply. When producers expect the price of a good or service to increase, they may reserve some of it at present and thus decrease supply. Conversely, when producers anticipate a price drop, they likely will flood the market with their product while prices are still relatively high.

INFLUENCES ON ELASTICITY OF SUPPLY

The degree to which a producer can change the means of production represents the main effect upon the elasticity of supply. In other words, if a producer easily can generate more or less of a product, then the supply will be more elastic. All industries have elastic supply given a long enough period, but only a few industries have elastic supply in the short term. For instance, a shoe company has to make major investments in labor, materials, and factory overhead in order to produce shoes. If the demand for shoes rises suddenly, it will not be easy for the company to create a correspondingly high supply overnight. In general, the supply of goods that require skilled labor and major capital investment is inelastic. On the other hand, supply can be elastic for a business that requires little capital and no skilled labor. A house cleaning service, for instance, can meet raise in demand almost immediately simply by hiring more employees.

MARKET EQUILIBRIUM

In general, market economies tend to move toward the point at which the quantity demanded at a certain price equals the amount supplied at that price. This movement occurs in all free markets: if the price is too high to attract the maximum number of buyers, the seller will lower it; if the demand is too great for a product at a certain price, the seller will raise the price. Over time, an equilibrium price is reached. Attaining an equilibrium price does not guarantee success for the seller, since the equilibrium price may be too low for profit to be possible. Nevertheless, the market will tend in this direction. As long as a difference exists between supply and demand, the market is said to be in disequilibrium.

Surpluses and Shortages

A market can be in disequilibrium in two major ways: surplus and shortage. When a surplus exists, the supply is greater than the demand. In a shortage, supply is less than demand. A surplus often results from high prices that drive down demand. A shortage, on the other hand, may result from low prices that cause the great demand to exceed supply. Maintaining a surplus can prove expensive for producers, since all of those goods have to be stored and maintained. Producers typically will lower the price until surplus is eliminated. In the case of a shortage, the producer will recognize that many people would buy the product even at a higher price. Then the producer likely will raise the price even though this action somewhat diminishes demand.

Price System

Increases in supply necessitate lower prices to generate sufficient demand. When many producers for a specific good or service exist, the supply will be greater and prices will be lower. Indeed, producers of the same good or service likely will engage in competitive pricing, meaning they will lower prices below equilibrium in order to attract their competitors' customers. This scenario is advantageous for customers, but it can prove destructive for profit margins. In a market economy, interplay between the desires of supplier and consumer tend to drive the price system. The price system in such an economy is flexible, insofar as structural changes in the market result in a change in price. Overall, the price system tends to be efficient in that prices will gravitate toward equilibrium.

Price Ceilings and Price Floors

In a free market, price is not restricted. However, sometimes the government decides that pricing for a certain good or service should be limited. A price ceiling sets an upper limit on the price of a good or service. Price ceilings are established below the equilibrium price, which creates a shortage. In other words, a price ceiling guarantees that demand exceeds supply. A price floor, on the other hand, sets a minimum price greater than equilibrium. This action guarantees a surplus, since supply will exceed demand. Minimum wage, a common example of a price floor, can be problematic since employers may be unwilling to pay the lowest-possible wage and may therefore fuel greater unemployment.

Perfect Competition

A free market strives for perfect competition, although markets rarely attain this state. In order for a market to have perfect competition, it must have multiple buyers and sellers so no one group can have total control over price. In order for these sellers to be equally powerful, their products must be identical. Otherwise, a disparity will exist in the demand for slightly different products. In addition, the buyers and sellers in a market of perfect competition must have the freedom to enter or exit the market as they please. Obligation to stay in the market creates opportunities for artificially high or low price. Participants in a market with perfect competition will be educated and capable of obtaining the best value. Finally, participants in a market with perfect competition will be independent: that is, they will not collude or cooperate to influence pricing.

Monopoly

A monopoly is a market with no competition that is controlled by one seller. A business that has a monopoly can set prices wherever it wants. Since no close substitutes for their product exist, buyers have no choice but to pay whatever price the seller establishes. Obviously, a monopoly is terrible for buyers, since they have no influence on pricing. For the most part, the government prohibits monopolies. However, in some industries the government allows a monopoly to exist because not enough room exists for multiple sellers. For instance, electricity providers often have a monopoly in certain areas, because maintaining multiple sets of infrastructure for providing electricity would not make sense. When this is the case, the government keeps a close eye on the monopoly to ensure that customers are not exploited.

Natural, Government, Technological, and Geographic

A natural monopoly develops when production inputs are lowest as long as only one seller exists. For instance, utility providers often have a natural monopoly because it would be horribly inefficient to have multiple sets of pipes and water treatment facilities run by competing businesses. A government monopoly exists when the government either runs the sole provider or allows only one provider to exist. The United States Postal Service is a good example of a government monopoly. A technological monopoly develops when only one firm has the means to create a certain product. For instance, a business that holds the patent on a manufacturing process will have a technological monopoly until the patent expires. A geographical monopoly occurs when only one business serves a particular area of the country or world. Some geographical markets simply are not large enough to support multiple sellers in a market.

Monopolistic Competition

Monopolistic competition is the predominant market structure, in which multiple sellers offer similar but not identical products. One example is the soft drink market, in which a number of slightly different products compete for the same customers. In a state of monopolistic competition, sellers work to differentiate their products with advertising. Where monopolistic competition exists, there are many sellers and many buyers, and so the incentive to carve out a brand identity is great. Sellers in this market have very little control over price, so they appeal to customers in other ways such as touting their materials, craftsmanship, or service, for example. Markets with monopolistic competition typically have small barriers to exit and entry, so businesses come and go frequently.

Oligopoly

An oligopoly is a market in which a relatively small number of sellers offer a similar product. Oligopolies are less competitive than markets of monopolistic competition, and sellers are better able to manipulate price. In an oligopoly, the sellers have less incentive to appeal to the buyers. Many oligopolies exist because risk associated with entry into the market is especially high. Automobile manufacturing, for instance, is extremely expensive, and so car companies do not emerge overnight. Only a few can exist at a given time, so those who survive have significant control over the market and price structures. The products in an oligopoly tend to be very similar, since there is little incentive for differentiation.

Antitrust Legislation

Since competition drives down prices and necessitates high marketing expenses, a lack of competition is often in the sellers' best interest. Sometimes, the sellers in a market form a trust to set prices and minimize competition. Of course, this strategy puts the customer at a great disadvantage, so the government has outlawed this practice. Specific antitrust legislation has been established to prevent large sellers from cooperating to reduce competition. For instance, the Sherman Antitrust Act of 1890 gave the federal government the right to break up or monitor monopolies, and more generally, to investigate attempts to reduce competition. Another way the government fights trusts is by forcing businesses to get permission before merging. In the past, businesses could join together and eliminate the need to compete with one another.

The United States government remains vigilant against business practices that reduce competition. Still, the government does not break up every monopoly; in some cases, the government allows a monopoly to exist under strict monitoring. The Department of Justice and the Federal Trade Commission are the bodies mainly responsible for antitrust enforcement. In particular, these departments spend a great deal of time investigating business mergers. As a result, these bodies prohibit mergers that will create an imbalance of power within a market. Businesses employ teams of lawyers to argue that their cooperation with others will not lead to a monopoly. At the same time, competitors not part of a planned merger will spend a great deal of money to prevent it from happening.

MARKET ALLOCATION, PRICE FIXING, AND PREDATORY PRICING

It is always in the interest of business to reduce competition. One way to accomplish this reduction is through market allocation, the intentional division of a market among competitors. For instance, competing businesses might agree to limit their sales to different geographic area in order to avoid paying for advertising and product differentiation in both areas. Another illegal way to reduce competition is price fixing, an agreement to establish prices at an artificially high level. As long as no competitors violate the agreement by lowering their prices, all the conspiring businesses can make unnaturally high profits. Finally, business sometimes will try to drive their competitors out of the market through predatory pricing, or the establishment of artificially low prices by large businesses able to afford short-term loss. Smaller businesses unable to afford the low price level will be forced to close.

GOVERNMENT PROTECTION OF CONSUMERS

The government tries to protect the interests of consumers by promoting competition whenever possible. The government institutes strict policies of public disclosure, and these policies force businesses to announce their actions and maintain transparency standards. Consumers are provided with whatever information they need to make an educated purchase. When a business is found violating the spirit of competition, the government may issue a cease and desist order requiring the business to terminate its activity immediately. The federal government also has established agencies responsible for regulating specific industries. The major federal consumer protection agencies are the Food and Drug Administration, Environmental Protection Agency, Consumer Product Safety Commission, Federal Trade Commission, Securities and Exchange Commission, and Federal Communications Commission.

GOVERNMENT DEREGULATION

Government regulation protects consumers, but it can also add unnecessary and crippling costs to businesses. Many administrations have sought to deregulate industry so the market can sort out the winners from the losers. Deregulation may have immediate benefits for consumers, as the increased competition drives prices down and forces businesses to innovate. However, deregulation entails less government oversight, so businesses may take actions that endanger the consumer and the environment. In recent years, the deregulation of the banking system has contributed to unwise financial practices culminating in the crisis of 2008. Deregulation can only work in the end if it is accompanied by strong oversight and ethical business practices.

Gross National Product

Gross national product is the sum total of government purchase of goods and services, consumption goods, gross private domestic investment goods, and exports. Total American domestic production is the value of final goods and services produced by American citizens anywhere in the world in one interval. Total domestic production is also known as total output. Government purchases of goods and services include all the non-capital and capital goods produced for governments at all levels, but exclude government spending. Gross national product is different than gross domestic product, or the value of all the goods and services produced in an economy over a certain period. GNP includes this value, but also includes the income earned by citizens through foreign investments.

GPDI

Gross private domestic investment (GPDI) goods are equal to the amount of new private capital produced, such as new residential building, new factories, and new equipment. This measure is one of the components of gross domestic product (GDP). GPDI includes the actual purchases by private individuals or firms of all goods that create some kind of return for the owners. This includes nonresidential investment, residential investment, and changes in inventory. GPDI is considered a good indicator of future economic success because it suggests the degree to which individuals and businesses are using their money to guarantee productivity down the road. In the United States, GPDI is typically between 15 and 18% of GDP.

Aggregate Income and Aggregate Demand

Aggregate income, also known as total income, is the total amount earned in the production of the gross domestic product. All the incomes in an economy combine to calculate aggregate income. The official tally for aggregate income does not include inflation or taxes. Aggregate demand, on the other hand, is the total amount of planned purchases and expenditures on goods and services at all income levels. Aggregate demand is also known as total costs, and it is calculated with the formula $AD = C + I + G (X - M)$, in which C is consumer spending on goods and services, I is business capital investment, G is government spending on public goods and services, X is exports of goods and services, and M is imports of goods and services.

Exogenous and Endogenous Variables

When considering the state of the economy, one must account for both exogenous and endogenous variables. An exogenous variable has a value that is not dependent on other economic variables, while an endogenous variable does depend on other economic factors. Consumer spending, for instance, is dependent on interest rates and income; therefore, consumer spending represents an endogenous variable. Consumer preference, on the other hand, cannot be explained through other economic indicators; therefore, consumer preference is an exogenous variable. In a model of supply and demand, changes in price are endogenous variables, while a political shift that affects demand is an exogenous variable.

Calculation of Savings and Disposable Income

Savings is calculated as disposable income less consumption expenditures. Disposable income, on the other hand, is calculated as income minus taxes. In essence, disposable income is the component of income over which the individual has full control. A person cannot choose whether to owe taxes, but he or she can decide whether to save income left after taxes or spend income left after taxes on television, groceries, or clothes. Any non-tax mandatory payments such as child support must be subtracted from disposable income, since such payments are not available for discretionary purchases.

Velocity of Money

The velocity of money is the frequency and rapidity with which people turn over their cash balances. Another way of looking at the velocity of money is as the median number of times a dollar is spent in a specific period of time. The velocity of money is calculated as $V = (P \times Q)/M$, in which P is the price level, Q is nominal GDP, and M is money supply. In other words, the velocity of money is the ratio of nominal GDP to the quantity of money in circulation. Proponents of the quantity theory of money believe that the velocity of money will be steady unless price level changes suddenly. A sharp increase in the velocity of money is thought to be a cause of inflation.

Monetarism

Monetarism, an economic theory, asserts that changes in the money supply will affect production and price level. Monetarists advocate adjustments in the money supply as the best way to manage the economy. Perhaps the most famous monetarist is Milton Friedman, who declared that expansion of the money supply was the predominant cause of inflation. Price level, therefore, is the most important economic indicator of the overall health of the economy. According to monetarism, the job of the central bank is to keep the money supply from expanding too much, while also maintaining sufficient liquidity to meet the needs of commercial banks. For a long time, monetarists believed that they had discovered the hidden rule of the economy, and that future management would be easy.

Money and Macroeconomic Activity

Monetarism from 1945 through the 1970s

After the Second World War, monetarism emerged as the dominant refinement of Keynesian economics. During the 1950s, most economists agreed that the expansion of the money supply would lead to increases in aggregate demand, while decreases in the money supply would lead to increases in investment. In other words, fluctuations in the money supply would be the primary determinant of private economic behavior. In the 1970s, monetarism seemed effective against stagflation; the Fed sought to limit the money supply and thus slowed down inflation. Although monetarism has not always been able to right a struggling economy, it has consistently stabilized prices.

Current attitude towards monetarism

In the past few decades, classical monetarism has failed to explain some of the most important economic events. For instance, in the 1990s the growth of the money supply was unrelated to inflation. Also, when the United States entered a minor recession in 2001, monetary policies had little effect. One of the reasons cited by economists for this failure is the stagnation of the retail sector. There is now some speculation that monetarism may have evaluated the role of government in battling inflation. Rather than adjusting the money supply in order to stave off monetary inflation, some economists believe that the government actually responds late to inflation in the commodity markets. Meanwhile, the Austrian School of economists criticizes monetarism for failing to consider the subjective value of money to the consumer.

Quantity theory of money and equations of exchange

The foundation of the quantity theory of money is the equation of exchange: MV = PY, in which M is the money supply, V is the velocity of money, P is the price level, and Y is the income/output level. Quantity theorists assume that velocity and income/output level are constant in the short term. As such, changes in the price level will mirror fluctuations in the money supply. Since the velocity of money only changes in response to long-term technological and political advances, and since wage and price adjustments keep output at roughly the same level, the only way to control inflation is to manage the money supply.

Adaptive expectations theory

The adaptive expectations theory asserts that individuals base their economic decisions on recent trends in financial indicators like interest rates. Individual investors assess the recent financial data and then make suppositions regarding future events. With this in mind, proponents of the adaptive expectations theory assert that only historical information should bear upon current concerns regarding monetary policy. One of the problems with adaptive expectations theory is its overemphasis on recent trends at the expense of a more long-term perspective. Adaptive expectations theory economists often are caught short when the recent past fails to explain current economic activity.

Asset demand theory of money demand

The asset demand theory of money demand, promoted by Milton Friedman, asserts that the demand for any assets, including money, depends upon the return on investment. This theory assumes that cash can earn interest such as in checking accounts. Proponents of this theory believe that individuals invest or save money based on not only their current income, but also based on their permanent income. If people perceive that bonds have a higher return on investment, then the demand for money will fall. Like many theories of money demand, the asset demand theory supposes excellent and accurate economic knowledge. For this reason, it is useful more as a benchmark against which to measure actual behavior.

PERMANENT INCOME

One of the major statistics economists consider in relation to the supply of money is permanent income. Economists define permanent income as the current value of an individual's anticipated lifetime earnings. Some economists believe that individual economic factors focus on their perception of permanent income when making purchasing, saving, and investing decisions. In fact, some people ignore temporary and short-term changes in income and instead rely on their perception of permanent income in order to decide what they can afford. One recent problem with the concept of permanent income is that people are much more likely now to change careers in mid-life. Such changes can exert significant impact perceptions of permanent income, and thus such career changes tend to weaken permanent income's influence on financial decisions.

EFFICIENT MARKET THEORY

One of the descendents of rational expectations theory is the efficient market theory. According to this theory, the price of financial assets will be based on the perspective of traders and all available information. The efficient market theory provides no special opportunities for extremely high returns. On occasion, individuals will be able to make large profits in a certain area, but the spread of information will bring prices back to normal soon. The efficient market theory largely depends upon economic behavior; although, critics argue that financial deregulation in the 1990s has enabled a global financial elite consistently to gain an intellectual advantage over the rest of the market. Many of the federal government's current regulatory efforts aim to reduce this advantage.

INVENTORY THEORY OF MONEY DEMAND

In the 1950s, James Tobin and William Baumol promoted the inventory theory of money demand. According to this theory, people obtain inventories of money in order to purchase goods and services in the future. Factors such as individual income, the cash-conversion fee, and interest rates influence whether this inventory converts into cash. Proponents of this theory assume that cash will earn zero interest and that bonds are risky investments. However, since United States Treasury bills are a no-risk investment, the availability of these bills belies such a claim. According to this theory, rational actors will diversify their holdings into cash and bonds.

CHANGES IN INTEREST RATES

According to the inventory theory of money demand, when interest rates are at 10 percent, rational actors will keep the majority of their wealth in bonds because they will expect rates to fall and enable them to make profits. However, when interest rates are a bit lower (such as at 8 percent), rational actors will put the majority of their wealth in cash, because they will expect rates to rise and make bonds less profitable. This theory suggests that the velocity of money will rise in an expanding economy and will decline in a contracting economy. Likewise, a rise in interest rates will raise the velocity of money, while a decline in interest rates will slow down the velocity of money. John Maynard Keynes reached these same conclusions.

LIQUIDITY PREFERENCE THEORY

MOTIVES FOR HOLDING ONTO LIQUID ASSETS

According to the liquidity preference theory promoted by John Maynard Keynes, three motives exist for holding onto liquid assets (Keynes equated liquid assets with cash and illiquid assets with bonds.). These three motives are the transaction motive, the speculative/portfolio motive, and the precautionary motive. The transaction motive is the desire to save money to pay for normal expenses like rent and food. The speculative motive, also known as the portfolio motive, is the desire to save money in case an investment opportunity arises. The precautionary motive is the desire to save money for medical expenses. A person's assessment of these three factors will determine whether he or she keeps money as cash or invests it as bonds.

ECONOMIC BEHAVIOR

According to the proponents of the liquidity preference theory, people either will put all their money in cash or invest it all in bonds, depending on whether they believe interest rates will rise or fall. If people expect interest rates to rise, they will keep their assets in cash. Conversely, if people expect interest rates to fall, they will purchase bonds. This idea supposes individuals' knowledge of the normal rate of interest to which they can compare changes in the actual rate. The proponents of this theory believe that the velocity of money would increase during an expanding economy and decrease during a contracting economy. Furthermore, they believe that the velocity of money would rise and fall along with interest rates.

MODERN KEYNESIAN APPROACH TO THE THEORY OF MONEY DEMAND

The modern Keynesian approach to the theory of money demand incorporates rational expectations theory and further suggests that workers and employees will demand a wage based on their rational expectations of economic conditions. Modern Keynesians emphasize the stickiness of wages and prices; namely, wages and prices are slow to respond to changes in supply and demand. An increased awareness of the imperfection of knowledge in financial decision-making has accompanied this trend. Modern Keynesians have a more tempered view of a government's potential to provide positive intervention in the economy.

MONEY DEMAND THEORY

Money demand theory, promoted by Irving Fisher, asserts that the velocity of money is affected by the number of pay periods every year, the speed of postal deliveries, and the availability of credit. In the short term, according to this theory, velocity of money and output are constants. For this reason, money demand = PY/V. In other words, P is proportional to M. If the money supply doubles, the price level also will double. In the short term, the demand for money is dependent on the price level and the income level of the individual, assuming that interest rates are not affecting the demand for money.

NEW CLASSICAL THEORY

The new classical theory of monetary policy is a refinement of the Keynesian perspective; it combines rational expectations theory with close analysis of policy decisions. This theory, also called the rational expectations equilibrium theory, emerged in the 1970s. It assumes pure competition and perfectly flexible wages and prices. According this theory's proponents, all unemployment is voluntary; in other words, all unemployed workers could find a job if they were willing to settle for a low enough wage. New classical theorists developed complex forecasts of the monetary policy pursued by the Federal Reserve. At the same time, they perform detailed analyses of the results of past decisions made by the Fed.

NEW CLASSICAL PERSPECTIVE ON MONETARY POLICY, WAGES, AND PRICES

New classical theorists do not believe that anticipated changes in monetary policy will affect unemployment; rather, these anticipated changes only will affect prices and the rate of inflation. However, unanticipated changes in monetary policy may result in short-term changes in real output and income. This idea depends on the concept of sticky prices, proposed by John Maynard Keynes, by which prices do not adjust quickly in order to equalize supply and demand. At the same time, wages are sticky because they are affected by long-term contracts and union deals. This combination of sticky wages and prices with rational expectations means that the money supply curve never will decrease as much as the new classical theorists suppose. In the short term, employment and output will rise, although new classical theorists would say it should go down.

QUANTITY THEORY OF MONEY

The quantity theory of money, first proposed by economists at Cambridge, asserts that income is the primary factor influencing the demand for money. Income connects to the amount of money people intend to spend. Quantity of money theorists use the equation money demand = k × Y, in which k is the income people wish to hold onto. Economists who take this view do not believe that moderate inflation or slight changes in the price level have a great impact on money demand. For the most part, these economists view perception of permanent income as the primary driver of monetary demand. Of course, persistent economic shocks and increasing unemployment can undermine the credibility of permanent income estimates.

RATIONAL EXPECTATIONS THEORY

According to rational expectations theory, as promoted by John F. Muth and Robert E. Lucas, individuals develop their expectations for market prices and return on investment from current and historical data. According to this theory, monetary policies do not exert effect on the economy, assuming that individuals use all of the available information and have rational expectations. Of course, this scenario never occurs in real life. Instead, this theory sets a benchmark against which actual behavior can be judged. Rational expectations theory does not permit a short-run Phillips curve, meaning that the theory does not account for the short-term inverse relationship between inflation and unemployment.

CRITICISMS

As the influence of rational expectations theory on monetary policy has grown, so have the criticisms of the theory. Many economists assert that no predictions about future economic activity can be accurate; moreover, obtaining enough information to make an accurate prediction would be expensive. Economic behavior tends to base on current status as well as the recent past, and such foundations do not necessarily make for wise decision-making. Another potential problem with rational expectations theory is that individual behavior does not always translate into the aggregate. For this reason, rational expectations theory is a poor microeconomic predictor. One of the recent trends in economic analysis has combined rational expectations theory with adaptive expectations theory, which takes into account changes in public perception of economic events. For instance, modern economists tend to adjust their models based on the perceived credibility of the federal government, whereas rational expectation theorists assume that the public takes the statements of the government at face value.

INFLATION

Inflation is a decline in the value of money or a rise in the level of prices. A few hypotheses attempt to establish the cause of inflation. One such hypothesis asserts that price levels rise along with increases in the money supply. Other economists, including Milton Friedman, believe that inflation can be held in check as long as the increase in the money supply is proportionate to the expansion of the economy. Still other economists assert that wage increases serve to raise the price of manufacturing and ultimately raise prices and cause inflation. Finally, structural theorists believe that problems with economic organization lead to inflation, often resulting in imbalanced trade with other nations. Inflation often causes a decline in the level of savings, as people want to spend their money before it loses its value.

Consumer Price Index

One of the common tools that economists use to measure inflation is the consumer price index. The consumer price index is a metric for analyzing fluctuations in the prices of goods and services purchased often by consumers. The first step in the creation of this index is surveying the American public to determine the most oft-purchased goods and services. The federal government selects a set of approximately 400 goods and services as the market basket. These goods and services are weighted according to their share of the household budget. Then, the government compiles monthly prices for all the market basket items and compares these prices in order to determine whether a significant long-term rise in price levels has occurred.

Producer Price Index

Economists use the consumer price index to gauge the effects of inflation on consumers. However, in order to measure the effects of inflation on producers they must use the producer price index. The producer price index is a metric of changes in the prices of wholesale goods. The system for deriving the producer price index is the same as the system for deriving consumer price index, except the producer price index pays greater attention to the price received for goods rather than the price paid for the same goods. In addition, economists often make different producer price indices for different industries or for different stages of production (such as for raw materials or finished goods).

Inflation Rate

Economists define the inflation rate as the rate of fluctuation in prices over a defined interval. Economists use both the producer price index and the consumer price index to calculate the inflation rate. Economists typically consider the inflation rate on either a monthly or an annual basis, although in cases of extreme inflation they might examine the rate on a weekly or daily basis. In the 1960s and 1970s, economists became convinced that inflation directly related to the money supply. However, in the 1990s the correlation between these two variables disappeared. Economists currently consider an inflation rate of between 1 and 3 percent annually as acceptable for the American economy.

Creeping Inflation, Galloping Inflation, Hyperinflation, and Deflation

Some fluctuation in prices and in the purchasing power of money in an economy is typical. Even in the American economy, considered one of the most stable in the world, there is between one and three percent inflation annually. When inflation increases gradually over a long period of time, economists refer to it as creeping inflation. If the inflation rate rises drastically, on the other hand, economists refer to it as galloping inflation. Hyperinflation is defined by economists as inflation of 50% or more every month. Economies that undergo hyperinflation become extremely unstable, and currency becomes almost worthless. Deflation, on the other hand, is any decrease in the purchasing power of money or in price levels. There was massive deflation in the United States during the Great Depression.

Demand-Pull Inflation

A number of economic factors can cause inflation. Sometimes, overall demand rises faster than production, which causes prices to rise and money to lose purchasing power. Economists describe such a scenario as demand-pull inflation. An economy is vulnerable to demand-pull inflation when positive events increase consumer confidence. In such an economy, typically a brief lag occurs while producers work to meet the rise in demand. During the lag period, prices rise. Furthermore, overabundance of money in the economy can also cause demand-pull inflation. For instance, if the

Federal Reserve puts too much money in the American economy, consumption will go up before production can increase to meet it.

Cost-Push Inflation and Wage-Price Spirals

Drastic rises in production costs result in increasing prices in a scenario called cost-push inflation. Sudden increases in energy cost or raw materials cost often causes cost-push inflation. Because of the United States' dependence upon petroleum, for instance, there is always a danger of cost-push inflation when oil prices rise. Increases in wages present another potential cause for cost-push inflation. If the increases in wages raise production costs, the resulting rise in prices can lead to demands for even higher wages. The resulting wage-price spiral can be very difficult to escape.

Effects of Inflation

Diminished Value of Currency

Inflation causes a number of problems, mainly because it injects uncertainty into economic decisions. Interestingly, an economy can handle a high rate of inflation as long as it is regular and predictable. Unfortunately, the rate of inflation is never foreseeable, so the declining purchasing power of the dollar has negative consequences. For instance, people who are on a fixed income or receive a stable wage will not be able to purchase as much with the same amount of money in the future. This is particularly a problem for senior citizens living on a fixed retirement income. On the other hand, inflation can be a boon to those who borrow money. The amount of money borrowed becomes easier to pay, because it is worth less than it was when it was borrowed. In some cases, an individual who borrows money at interest can actually make a net profit in value if inflation diminishes the value of currency.

Diminished Rate of Return on Savings

Inflation can have devastating effects on the rate of return on savings. Savings accounts with a fixed rate of interest continue to generate the same amount of money, but this money has decreasing value. Even though inflation tends to increase the amount of money saved, the loss in value offsets this increase. When inflation becomes significant, citizens may prove hesitant to save their money, since they perceive the money will have considerably less value in the future. Instead, these consumers may elect to spend their money while it still has some value. In other words, the diminished rate of return on savings caused by inflation can lead to unnecessary purchases and profligacy.

Increased Interest Rates

When inflation causes prices to increase, interest rates generally increase as well. Lending institutions will raise interest rates to ensure continued profit despite drops in the value of currency. For borrowers, obtaining a loan becomes more expensive. High interest rates discourage businesses from borrowing money to make large-scale improvements and major purchases. At the same time, consumers are reluctant to finance (that is, buy with a series of small payments) large items. All of these factors suggest that inflation can be crippling to economic development.

Monetary Policy in the United States

Taylor Rule for Setting Interest Rates

Governments manipulate interest rates in order to achieve their inflation targets. The Taylor rule, created by the American economist John Taylor, is one tool for determining the appropriate interest rate to keep inflation stable. According to the Taylor rule, the government should increase interest rates when inflation is high, and should lower interest rates when inflation is low. The Taylor rule also considers employment statistics; it recommends increasing interest rates when unemployment is low and lowering interest rates when unemployment is high. Although the Fed's decisions tend to agree with Taylor rule recommendations, the Fed has never declared allegiance to the rule.

Monetary System

The monetary system is composed of the Federal Reserve and all of the banks that accept deposits and allow individuals and businesses to send and receive payments. The Federal Reserve is responsible for establishing the rules that govern the behavior of banks. Three basic kinds of financial institution accept deposits and therefore comprise the monetary system: commercial banks, thrift institutions, and money market funds. Commercial banks receive their authority, either by the Comptroller of the Currency in the United States Treasury or by a state agency, to make loans and receive deposits. Thrift institutions include savings and loan associations, savings banks, and credit unions. Money market funds sell shares and use the money they acquire to obtain assets.

Creation of Liquidity

One of the valuable functions that the monetary system's institutions perform is the creation of liquidity. An asset is liquid when easily converted into money and used to make payments. For instance, a block of gold has immense value, but converting a gold block into an equivalent amount of currency for buying groceries is difficult. Banks and other institutions in the monetary system are able to create liquid assets by making loan commitments over a long period and accepting deposits over a relatively short period. Because banks charge a higher interest rate for loans than they give for deposits, they make money in the end and avoid having to call in loans unexpectedly.

Lowered Cost

Commercial banks and other financial institutions that make up the monetary system reduce the costs of borrowing and lending funds. Banks offer a wide variety of deposits and loans to customers who would otherwise have to search high and low to find a match for their financial needs. Accordingly, the cost of doing financial business is lower in terms of both monetary expense and time. Having one centralized location for borrowing and lending funds allows consumers to obtain a wide variety of services. In addition, the liquidity safeguard provided by the monetary system helps banks and other financial institutions avoid unfavorable lending situations. Both intermediaries and depositors can obtain sufficient liquidity relatively easily.

Mitigation of Risk

One of the advantages that the financial institutions in the monetary system create is the mitigation of risk. Inevitably, some loans will remain unpaid. However, an institution like a bank makes so many loans over such a long period of time that the damage done by a few unpaid loans is very small. Moreover, a bank can create a knowledge base over a long period of time in order to set interest rates that ensure profitability. This kind of precision would prove impossible for an institution that only made a few loans a year. A bank charges high enough interest rates to pay off the cost of unpaid loans.

The banks and other financial institutions that make up the monetary system make it easy for individuals and businesses to make payments and transfer funds. Instead of acquiring hard currency and physically moving it from one place to another, depositors can write checks or use credit and debit cards to move funds. The network of communication required to handle all of the checks written in the United States is incredibly complex, so it is valuable to have institutions whose explicit job is to handle these transactions. Banks can charge small fees for some transactions such as those transactions involving credit cards.

Deposit Multiplier Formula and Fractional Reserve Banking

Using the deposit multiplier formula, economists can estimate how much a cash deposit will increase the money supply. The deposit multiplier formula is 1/required reserve ratio. Therefore, the larger the required reserve ratio, the more money that cash deposit will create. As an example, if the required reserve ratio is 20 percent, then every dollar deposited can yield five dollars of usable funds. In other words, producing a large sum for economic use takes a relatively small sum. This system, in which banks keep only a portion of deposits on hand, constitutes fractional reserve banking. Most developed economies have fractional reserve banking, a system that necessitates a strong central bank.

Influences on the Demand for Money

Income Level

Income levels have a major impact on the demand for money. When income levels increase, businesses and people retain more money. Accordingly, income levels increase along with demand. Individuals and businesses tend to keep more money because they feel they are more likely to be making purchases. Assuming that interest rates are relatively stable, individuals and businesses will not increase the proportion of their income that goes toward investment. When the demand for money increases due to expanded income, the Fed usually will introduce more money into the American economy. However, the Fed must be careful not to encourage inflation by introducing too much money into the economy.

Cost of Goods and Services

If the costs of goods and services increase, a greater demand for money generally ensues. Consumers will recognize that products and services are more expensive, and those consumers will need to withdraw more money in order to pay for their daily expenses. Not just true of individual consumers, this principle also is true businesses, which need to keep a certain amount of cash on hand in order to maintain operations. If the business is required to pay more for goods and services, it may have to raise prices in order to keep up with expanding production costs, thus exacerbating the need for more money in the economy.

Interest Rates

Interest rates have a great impact on the demand for money. When interest rates are high, the demand for money tends to decrease, because high interest rates tend to lure individuals and businesses to place more money in savings instruments. Whenever interest rates rise, greater investment in stocks, bonds, and savings accounts occurs. Investors want to take advantage of the increased yields available because of the higher interest rates. When people invest money, that money is taken out of circulation. However, if interest rates drop individuals and businesses will spend their money rather than save it and the demand for money will increase. In such situations, businesses and individuals perceive that investing money presents little gain.

M1

M1, also known as transactions money, consists of cash and checkable deposits. M1 is not the entirety of the money supply, but it does constitute a significant component. Individuals and businesses use M1 to make routine transactions. Sometimes when people need more access to cash in checkable deposits, the demand for money will rise. For instance, during the summer and during the holiday season people tend to make more purchases, so the Fed will increase the cash reserves at banks. Because this increase in the money supply is only temporary, it does not tend to lead to real inflation.

FLUCTUATIONS IN CURRENCY DEMAND DURING DIFFERENT PARTS OF THE WEEK OR MONTH

Currency demand varies slightly during different parts of the week or month, and government economists have become adept at manipulating the money supply in order to take advantage of these anticipated trends. Economists have noted that the supply of cash in circulation is greater at the beginning of the week because individuals have had the entire weekend to withdraw money from automated teller machines. In the past, individual depositors would have only been able to withdraw their money during the week and during bank hours. In addition, there tends to be more money in the financial system towards the beginning of the month, since many people receive wages at the first of the month.

FEDERAL FUNDS RATE

The federal funds rate is the rate of interest at which one bank can lend reserve funds to another or overnight. The federal funds in question are the reserves that banks have deposited with the Federal Reserve. Since banks do not receive interest while their funds are deposited with the Fed, banks often loan these funds to one another. . Further, banks commonly engage in these transactions in order to satisfy the reserve requirements. The Fed attempts to adjust the federal funds rate by purchasing and selling government bonds. For instance, the Fed will buy bonds in order to achieve a lower target for the federal funds rate. Conversely, the Fed will sell bonds in order to achieve a higher federal funds rate.

PRIME RATE

The best interest rate that banks charge customers is the prime rate. Banks offer the prime rate to customers who have excellent credit ratings or have a long history with the bank. Other borrowers likely will pay two or three percent more than the prime rates. Offering all loans at the prime rate would not be profitable for a bank. The prime rate is tied directly to the discount rate charged by the Fed. The Fed often considers the prime rate banks offer before making major adjustments to the discount rate. For one thing, the Fed will try not to establish a discount rate that leaves banks at a great disadvantage relative to prime rate loans already made.

MONEY MULTIPLIER

Economists use the money multiplier to estimate the effect of changes in the money supply of various acts of monetary policy. The money multiplier is calculated as the money supply divided by the monetary base. In other words, the money multiplier is the change in the money supply for each dollar of change in the monetary base. As an example, if the multiplier is 2.5, then a $1 million increase in the monetary base will lead to a $2.5 million increase in the money supply, since the same money can appear in multiple places in the economy. For instance, when a customer takes a loan from the bank and uses the money to make capital improvements, the money exists both as a bank asset and as expenditure in the real economy.

Basic Fiscal Policy

Fiscal policy is the action taken by the government to influence the economy by raising or lowering government spending and taxes. For instance, if the government wants to stimulate economic activity, it implements expansionary fiscal policy specifically by increasing spending or reducing taxes. Usually, expansionary policy creates an increased gross domestic product and higher price levels. Conversely, the government may want to use restrictive fiscal policy in an effort to slow the economy. Restrictive fiscal policy generally consists of decreasing spending or increasing taxes, resulting in gross domestic product decreases and lower price levels.

Basic Monetary Policy

The Federal Reserve System uses monetary policy to influence the money supply. The Fed has three tools at its disposal when creating monetary policy. The Fed can adjust the required reserve ratio, or the minimum amount a bank can have in its reserves. When this ratio is lowered, the money supply tends to increase. The Fed's most powerful tool is its open market operations, in which it buys and sells government securities, depending on whether it wants to remove or add money to circulation. The Fed can also manipulate the money supply by adjusting the discount rate, the rate charged to member banks when they borrow money from the Fed. Obviously, a favorable discount rate will encourage banks to borrow more money and put it into circulation.

Discretionary Fiscal Policy

Any act of fiscal policy voluntarily undertaken by the government is discretionary fiscal policy. For instance, the government must make specific decisions regarding taxation and spending every year. These decisions have a direct impact on the economy. For this reason, discretionary fiscal policy is a controversial subject; many conservative economists believe that the government should interfere with the economy as little as possible. Indeed, such an attitude prevailed among government economists until the Great Depression, when unemployment and economic stagnation hit historic highs. This crisis led many economists, most notably John Maynard Keynes, to rethink government intervention and ultimately to advocate direct stimulation of demand. Since then, the United States government has been less reticent to use fiscal policy as a means of stimulating demand and thereby reducing unemployment.

Automatic Stabilizers

Progressive Income Tax

The central tools of discretionary fiscal policy are the automatic stabilizers of progressive income taxation and public transfer payments. These tools, deemed automatic stabilizers, naturally exert either expansionary or contractionary influences upon the economy, depending on the current economy's needs in order to become stable. An income tax is as progressive when the rate of taxation increases in proportion to income. In other words, a millionaire pays a greater percentage of her earnings in taxes than does a minimum wage employee. The progressive income tax restrains the expansion of the economy by taking away a greater percentage of earnings from those persons who earn the most and who would otherwise feed their earnings back into the economy in the form of spending or investment. On the other hand, when the economy struggles, people earn less money and therefore pay less in taxes, which helps them survive the tough times.

Public Transfer Payments

Public transfer payments include unemployment benefits, food stamps, welfare, and other government entitlement programs. These payments are automatic stabilizers because they naturally counteract the movement of the economy. When the economy thrives, fewer people qualify for unemployment and other benefits, so the government spends less on these programs. To the extent that the government feeds less money into the economy, there is less stimulation of aggregate demand, so the expansion of the economy is restrained. However, when the economy is down, more people qualify for benefits. As a result, the government feeds more money into the economy. This government action stimulates aggregate demand and improves consumer spending, thus helping the economy recover. Automatic stabilizers like public transfer payments help the economy because they exert a leveling influence no matter what the circumstances.

Expansionary Fiscal Policy

The general purpose of expansionary fiscal policy is to stimulate a struggling economy. Increasing government spending and decreasing taxes are the two basic strategies of expansionary fiscal policy. During a recession, a government often increases its spending on infrastructure and other projects. This increase creates jobs during a time of higher unemployment and increases aggregate demand. When aggregate demand improves, prices rise and businesses feel more comfortable investing in long-term capital improvements. In turn, this improvement creates more jobs and increases GDP. Likewise, if the government decides to cut taxes, then individuals and business will have more money to invest and spend. Again, unemployment will reduce and GDP will improve. Most of the time, the practice of expansionary fiscal policy involves a combination of tax cuts and government spending.

Contractionary Fiscal Policy

The main purpose of contractionary fiscal policy is to restrain a rapidly growing economy and thereby to restrain inflation. The government wants to decrease aggregate demand so that it does not outpace aggregate supply and create scarcity issues and dramatic rises in the price level. The two main strategies of contractionary fiscal policy are to raise taxes and to decrease government spending. Both of these actions remove money from the economy either by taking more away as tax or by reducing the amount spent on government projects. As a result, people and businesses have less money to spend and invest, and the expansion of the economy slows. Businesses react to these trends by slowing production, and the reduction in demand quells inflation.

Problems with Fiscal Policy

While fiscal policy makes good theoretical sense, it presents some practical problems. First, discretionary policy decisions never occur because of perfect knowledge, so there is always the chance of making the wrong decision. Fiscal policy may take too long to develop and enact, and this lag time may reduce efficacy. More generally, governments have a hard time coordinating policy implementation with the business cycle. For example, an expansionary policy implemented during a time of inflation may prove disastrous. Another problem concerns economic actor's high levels of awareness and knowledge regarding government fiscal policy. Naturally these individuals and businesses will take steps to preserve their own interests in the anticipated economic climate. If people assume that expansionary fiscal policy will cause inflation, then they may decide to spend their money while it still has value. Unfortunately, this increase in spending only contributes to increased inflation. Finally, a country as large and varied as the United States may find it hard to construct a one-size-fits-all fiscal policy.

Keynesian Fiscal Policy

John Maynard Keynes developed his fiscal policy ideas in the wake of the Great Depression, when economists were searching desperately for a way to stimulate the economy. Keynes emphasized aggregate demand as the biggest influence on the business cycle, and he especially focused on investment as the main driver of aggregate demand. He often cited the spending multiplier effect, by which a dollar invested has a disproportionate influence on GDP. He believed that the government should stimulate aggregate demand by investing money in infrastructure and other projects. Accordingly, Roosevelt's New Deal program featured thousands of small and large projects funded by government investment. Most economists credit this government investment with reducing unemployment, reviving the economy, and restoring faith in American business.

ROLE OF GOVERNMENT IN DEMAND-SIDE ECONOMICS

Ever since Keynes, it has been assumed that the government will spearhead demand-side fiscal policy. That is, the government usually raises or lowers aggregate demand by adjusting taxes and spending. Most economists believe that the government can reduce unemployment and pull an economy out of recession by increasing spending and decreasing taxes. However, critics have observed that once government spending begins, it is difficult to stop. The public grows accustomed to federal programs, and terminating those programs in times of economic expansion causes the government great cost. In addition, unmonitored increases in government spending can lead to inflation. One scenario in which demand-side policies seem powerless is stagflation, such as that experienced by the United States during the late 1970s.

SUPPLY-SIDE ECONOMICS

Supply-side economics emphasizes policies that increase aggregate supply. Whereas demand-side economists advocate government intervention in the economy (through changes in taxation and spending), supply-siders generally want the government to stay out of business. By reducing taxes and regulation, the government can encourage business investment and production. In turn, this approach will allow businesses to grow and provide more jobs. In particular, supply-side economists believe that the rich should pay very little taxes, so they can use their earnings to create more jobs and better businesses. Supply-side economics is sometimes called "trickle down economics," because it assumes that economic benefits will descend from the upper income brackets to the lower income brackets. However, some critics assert that reducing taxes on the rich does not create a proportionate number of new jobs, while other critics contend that government deregulation of business leads to abuses of power and unethical behavior.

LAFFER CURVE

The Laffer Curve is an oft-cited demonstration of how tax cuts affect tax revenues. As such, the Laffer Curve is a graph with tax rate on the x-axis and revenue on the y-axis. The curve on the graph is an inverted U: it goes up for a while, then peaks and descends. For supply-side economists, the Laffer Curve is proof that increasing tax rates can actually diminish the amount of money collected by the government. According to the model, tax rates only can increase so much before they begin to discourage individuals and businesses from earning. In other words, excessively high taxes will dissuade people from working, so they will earn less money and actually pay less in taxes. If tax rates fall, on the other hand, people are more motivated to work and earn taxable income, so the amount of tax revenue actually can rise with a decrease in the tax rate.

PRACTICAL EFFECTS

The implementation of supply-side policies in the 1980s went largely according to plan. A reduction in tax rates, particularly for upper-income brackets, actually produced more tax revenue. The economy continued to expand, with low unemployment and inflation rates. However, the supply-side predictions regarding productivity did not all come true: for instance, many people declined to work more simply because they would keep a greater percentage of their earnings. In addition, people saved less of the money they earned than Laffer and other economists had predicted. Some economists believe that supply-side economics can be damaging if implemented at the wrong time. For instance, if the economy is on the left side of the Laffer Curve, a decrease in tax rates would not have a positive effect on tax revenue.

Federal deficit

When the government develops fiscal policy, it must take into consideration the effect on the federal balance sheet. When the government's revenues are greater than its expenses in a given year, a budget surplus occurs; when the opposite is true, there is a budget deficit. The full amount that the federal government owes is the national debt. Large federal deficits are bad for a number of reasons. For one thing, they require the federal government to borrow from other countries, which could put the United States at a diplomatic disadvantage. A large federal deficit also creates political opposition to further spending due to legitimate concerns regarding waste and profligacy. When a government runs a large federal deficit, the options for economic intervention become limited.

Causes

In general, create government might create a federal deficit for four reasons. In some cases, a federal deficit arises out of necessity, such as the case of a national emergency. During a war or natural disaster, the government must spend whatever is necessary to ensure the safety and prosperity of the nation. Economists may believe that a federal deficit is an unfortunate byproduct of necessary government spending during an economic downturn. Government spending on public goods, like roads and bridges, may not be necessary, but many people consider such spending worthwhile. . Finally, a federal deficit may be caused by government programs like Medicare, Social Security, and welfare. The necessity of these programs is a subject of great debate, though polls indicate that a majority of the population supports these programs.

Deficit spending

Deficit spending occurs when government expenses exceed government revenues in a budgetary year. An obvious question arises: how does the government fund deficit spending? The largest source of funds for the federal government is foreign investment. The United States also generates income for deficit spending by selling government securities like Treasury notes, bills, and bonds. These sales are really loans from the investor, since the government eventually will have to redeem the value of the security. Again, foreign governments such as Japan and China hold the largest number of United States securities. Nonetheless, American businesses and banks hold many of these securities as well.

National debt

When the federal government runs a consistent budget deficit, it accumulates a national debt. This debt consists of all the money owed to bondholders, as well as money borrowed from trust funds like Social Security, Medicare, and government pension funds. These programs often run up surpluses, and the federal government borrows their excess funds to pay for spending in other areas. Some economists do not consider money borrowed from government trust funds to be a part of the national debt, since it is a transfer of money from one part of the government to another. Many nations have considerable debt, and the negative consequences of doing so may not be so severe. A seemingly large debt is less of a problem if GDP is also high. For this reason, many economists focus on national debt as a percentage of GDP rather than simply looking at the size of the debt.

Although most people reflexively dislike the idea of a national debt, excessive government spending can have the positive effect of stimulating the economy in times of recession. Sometimes, though, excessive government spending crowds out private spending, and so the expenditures lack a viable point. . In other words, sometimes the government spends money that individuals and businesses would have spent anyway. This diminishes productivity and slows economic expansion. A large national debt creates negative perception of the economy and thereby diminishes investment and saving. For this reason, the federal government often takes steps to limit spending and pay down the national debt. Unfortunately, although most people support the idea of decreasing the debt in theory, there is considerable outcry when the government tries to eliminate specific programs.

American Economy and the Consumption of Foreign Goods

The health of the American economy connects with the consumption of foreign goods in the American market. When the American economy expands, prices within the United States increase and people tend to buy more foreign goods. This leads to increases in income and output abroad. When the American dollar appreciates, Americans buy more goods from overseas since these goods are cheaper. At the same time, a strong dollar means that exports will be more expensive for foreign citizens, and so international markets may purchase fewer American goods. The decline in American manufacturing has elevated consumption of foreign goods despite expansion of the economy.

The International Monetary System

Bretton Woods Agreement

The Bretton Woods agreement was in effect from 1944 to 1971. It stipulated that the United States must maintain a fixed price of gold relative to the dollar. Other countries could then peg their exchange rates to the dollar, which would be relatively stable. This agreement motivated the creation of the World Bank and the International Monetary Fund. There was occasionally concern about devaluation of the dollar, which created some problems for international central banks. Additional concern existed regarding the ability of the United States to protect the dollar. The Bretton Woods agreement was abandoned in 1973, when the United States ended the fixed rate system and stopped converting dollars to gold. At this point, the United States converted to flexible exchange rates.

GATT

In 1947, twenty two nations established the General Agreement on Tariffs and Trade (GATT), and it continued to influence international trade until 1995. The GATT was one of the byproducts of the creation of the United Nations. The intention of the agreement was to minimize tariffs and prevent weaker nations from unfair treatment in international trade. The GATT also sought to eliminate import quotas as a means of protecting domestic industry. When import quotas were unavoidable, the GATT preferred that this be accomplished through tariffs. Countries were forced to agree to a tariff schedule limiting the duties that could be levied on particular goods. The GATT also introduced most favored nation policies, through which tariffs could be reduced. Ultimately, the 1995 development of the World Trade Organization rendered the GATT obsolete.

MFN Status

One of the byproducts of the General Agreement on Tariffs and Trade (GATT) was most favored nation (MFN) status, used to restrict tariffs. The granting of MFN status to another country is a positive way of improving trade relations. For instance, the United States has designated China as a most favored nation in order to maintain excellent trade relations, even though the United States disapproves of some Chinese policies. Once a country receives MFN status, it must receive the same trade advantages as any other nation. This policy results in quick extension of bilateral trade agreements to many different countries. Third world and developing countries typically receive MFN status more easily than established countries, since it is believed to be in the interests of the developed world to help these fledgling economies grow.

American Reaction to Trade Deficit in the 1980s

Between 1982 and 1989, although the United States had a high level of imports, the US did not export at the same high rate. . In other words, the United States had a large foreign trade deficit. This trade deficit actually began in the 1960s, but it began to balloon out of control in the 1980s. For the most part, American economists dismissed the growing trade deficit as unimportant. They argued that much of the money spent by the United States abroad eventually came back and that the deficit would only be a problem if the dollar began to weaken. This view has been mostly vindicated, although in 2007, the American dollar lost a significant amount of its value relative to other currencies. According to Friedman and other economists, in a global economy based on floating exchange rates, such a situation is expected. Still, it remains to be seen whether the American manufacturing base is capable of generating sufficient exports to restore the strength of the dollar.

BALANCE OF PAYMENTS

The balance of payments is the flow of funds from the United States to other countries. This includes transactions made by governments as well as transactions made by private citizens and businesses. Tourism, imports, and foreign lending are among the transactions included in the balance of payments summary. Some analysts divide balance of payments into two categories: current accounts (interest payments, overseas profits, tourism, and imports/exports) and capital accounts (international bank deposits, investment, and debt securities). When a nation receives more money than it sends out, its currency tends to appreciate. Countries that find themselves with a large payment deficit often must export gold or other universally accepted currencies in order to settle their debts, since their imbalanced trade situation has reduced confidence in their national currency.

CURRENT AND CAPITAL ACCOUNTS IN INTERNATIONAL TRADE

Economists consider both the current and capital accounts in their analysis of international trade. The current account is the record of purchases and sales of securities and assets. Payments made to the United States (or to American businesses and government entities) exist on the positive side of the ledger, while payments to other countries exist on the negative side of the ledger. . The capital account, on the other hand, is the record of imports as compared to exports. Imports are money flowing out of the United States, while exports are the money coming in. A deficit exists when the United States has more imports than exports.

FOREIGN EXCHANGE MARKET

Currencies are bought and sold on the foreign exchange market, the largest market in the world. The foreign exchange market is an over-the-counter market, which means it is not located in any particular place. The market exists to make international trade easier by allowing trading partners to do business in the currency of their choice. If, for instance, an American company wants to make a purchase in Japanese yen, it can use dollars to obtain that currency in the foreign exchange market. The foreign exchange market is almost perfectly competitive, although strong central banks can manipulate it to a certain extent. Accordingly, the foreign exchange market is the most liquid market in the world. It has existed in its present incarnation since the transition from fixed exchange rates to floating rates.

FORWARD TRANSACTIONS AND SPOT TRANSACTIONS

Forward transactions are currency sales scheduled for some future date. Both sides in the deal agree to a set exchange rate prior to the transaction. In some cases, forward transactions are scheduled years ahead of time, and even wild swings in currency value do not affect the terms of the agreement. Trading partners use forward transactions to lock in preferable prices while they exist. A spot transaction, on the other hand, is a more immediate currency sale. Most spot transactions take two business days to complete. Spot transactions do not include interest, and they are completed with cash rather than with a contract. Because of their relative convenience, spot transactions are among the most common deals in the foreign exchange market.

FIXED EXCHANGE RATE, FLOATING EXCHANGE RATE, CREEPING/CRAWLING PEG SYSTEM, AND MANAGED FLOATING EXCHANGE RATE

International trade can be based on a number of different exchange rates. In a fixed exchange rate, the government pegs the rate at a certain level. Such pegging occurs when fears about rapid fluctuation in the exchange rate create an obstacle to trade. In a floating exchange rate, the rate is based on the supply and demand of a particular currency. In a creeping/crawling peg system, the Fed targets a short-term specific exchange rate and frequently adjusts the rate. A managed floating exchange rate combines floating and fixed systems. The exchange rate is not pegged, but in the short term a central bank may influence it.

International Monetary Fund

The International Monetary Fund was created to assure countries' compliance with the Bretton Woods agreement. Further, the IMF was intended to help countries solve the balance of payment problem. The IMF seeks to maintain stability in global trade and in the international monetary system. Also, the organization helps establish a payment system for transactions involving multiple countries. One of the ways the IMF seeks to manage developing economies is by suppressing their imports and encouraging their exports. Also, the IMF closely supervises debtor nations to make sure they are taking all necessary steps to repay what they owe without sacrificing economic development.

WTO

The World Trade Organization (WTO), established in Geneva in 1995, succeeded the General Agreement on Tariffs and Trade as the body in charge of reducing barriers to trade. Accordingly, the WTO moderates international disputes, trains financial professionals in developing markets, and monitors tariffs. The WTO also hosts meetings to work out trade agreements for the future. Over 150 nations belong to the World Trade Organization, and their contributions keep it in business. The efforts of the WTO have made it much easier for multinational corporations to enter foreign markets. Critics of the WTO charge that it exists to reinforce unfair trade arrangements pays lip service to human rights without offering substantial aid to impoverished nations.

The Bank for International Settlements

The Bank for International Settlements serves over 140 financial institutions, including central banks and other international monetary institutions. The BIS does not serve private individuals or corporations. This organization began in 1930 in accordance with the Treaty of Versailles (which concluded World War I). Since then, the primary goals of the BIS have been to regulate the valuation of equity and to encourage cooperation with regard to reserve requirements. The organization has established a minimum capital/asset ratio for central banks, and it is constantly monitoring reserve requirements to ensure they are in line with stability standards. The Bank for International Settlements is headquartered in Basel (Switzerland), although it has offices in Mexico City and Hong Kong.

Legal Frameworks for International Trade

Several major trade agreements were established in the twentieth century, thereby reducing obstacles to international commerce. The general model for all of these legal frameworks has been the General Agreement on Tariffs and Trade. The North American Free Trade Agreement (NAFTA) has opened trade between Canada, the United States, and Mexico since 1994. NAFTA eliminated tariffs and enabled American and Canadian companies to manufacture their goods in Mexico. In 1991, Russia and some of the former Soviet republics including Armenia, Georgia, Kazakhstan, and Ukraine, formed another trade association. This agreement has struggled in recent years because of simmering tensions between the member nations. One of the lessons of the CIS is that trade agreements are only as strong as the political relationships between the signatories.

Law of One Price

According to the law of one price, the prices of the same good in different locations will eventually equalize, since people search for the best price and competing sellers arrive at the lowest price that guarantees their profit. The law of one price seems to work especially well in the commodities and derivatives markets. The law of one price does not work in situations in which buyers have imperfect knowledge, since they will be unable to find the best price. In such situations, some sellers may maintain an artificially high price and count on less frequent but more lucrative sales.

Nominal and Real Exchange Rates

Economists must consider both the nominal and real exchange rates when evaluating international trade. The nominal exchange rate is the exchange rate between two countries when the price is not considered. In other words, the nominal exchange rate is a comparison of present market values. The real exchange rate, on the other hand, considers prices by measuring the purchasing power of each currency for both domestic and foreign goods and services. Nominal exchange rate, then, is useful for obtaining an approximate picture of currency strength, but in order to answer questions about specific products, economists must use the real exchange rate.

PPP, Absolute PPP, and Relative PPP

Purchasing power parity (PPP) is a measure used to determine whether a currency is overvalued or undervalued. Ideally, the price of a good should be the same in different countries. Absolute PPP does not take into account taxes, tariffs, and transportation costs. By this measure, the price of goods in the United States should be the same as the price of goods in other countries multiplied by the spot exchange rate. Relative PPP, on the other hand, compares the inflation rates in two countries to the exchange rate changes. The changes in the price and exchange rates should be proportional.

Interest Rate Parity Theory

Economists use the interest rate parity theory to explain the relationships between interest rates in trading countries. According to this theory, the exchange rate will adjust in the short term until the return on investment of domestic assets equals the return on investment of foreign assets. The theory suggests that the interest rate will equal the difference between the forward exchange rate and the spot exchange rate. American currency will appreciate in the following scenarios: when interest rates rise in the United States, when interest rates in other countries fall, when American income falls, when the exchange rate falls, when foreign income rises, when the United States sells foreign currency for dollars, and when foreign governments buy dollars with their currencies.

World Bank

The World Bank (shorthand for International Bank for Reconstruction and Development) was established at the Bretton Woods Conference in 1944. The World Bank loans funds to developing countries to pay for long-term capital improvements. At the time, it was mainly concerned with financing the recoveries of Europe and Asian economies ravaged by the Second World War. Now, the World Bank focuses on developing economies in Latin America, Africa, and Eastern Europe. The World Bank loans vast amounts of money at low interest rates, but it also deploys teams of economic advisers to provide assistance and monitor development efforts. Funding for the World Bank comes from donations by member nations and from the sale of bonds. The board of directors consists of one member from each of the 179 member nations.

European Economic Community

The European Economic Community (EEC; often called the Common Market) was established in 1957 to lower trade barriers between the nations of Western Europe, and in effect to turn these nations into a single market. The original member nations (Belgium, Holland, France, Italy, West Germany, and Luxembourg) sought to reduce competition, improve commercial transportation, and standardize trade policy. The result was a rapid expansion of trade and prosperity relative to non-member European nations. In time, the agreement would come to include other powers of the region, including Spain and Britain. Europe has turned into a single market close in size to the

United States. In 1993, the EEC became simply the European Community, and is at present administrated as part of the European Union.

Banker's Acceptance

The banker's acceptance is the form of bank draft that is most often used by importers and exporters. In this arrangement, a bank accepts a small fee and promises to make a payment on behalf of another business, typically one located outside of the country of the bank. Banker's acceptances can also be securitized and sold in money market funds. Some banks will purchase the acceptances of other banks just before they are due in order to increase liquidity. The secondary market is good for banker's acceptances at present, since the reserves of the selling bank guarantee these securities. At the same time, the stability of these securities makes international trade more possible.

DSST Practice Test

1. The single most important defining characteristic of money is:

a. that it is a commodity.
b. that it be issued in various denominations.
c. that it be fungible.
d. that it be acceptable by parties in trade.

2. Which of the following statements is FALSE with regard to "fiat money"?

a. Fiat money is used in the US instead of gold- or silver-backed currency.
b. Fiat money is essentially a promise and guarantee of value by a bona fide government.
c. Fiat money is pegged to and can be exchanged for either gold or silver.
d. Fiat money allows a government to more easily control the money supply.

3. A certificate that obligates the exchange of a specific weight of silver is an example of:

a. commodity money.
b. representative money.
c. fiat money.
d. paper money.

4. Aside from being a medium of exchange, money is often said to be a "unit of account." This means:

a. that money can be used as a measurement of the value and cost of ownership or operation.
b. that the value of money is determined by the things it can buy.
c. that money is denominated into various sectional units representing different values.
d. that the value of a unit of money expands or contracts according to the general economy.

5. Which of the following types of financial instruments is NOT a time deposit?

a. A one-month CD guaranteeing an annual interest rate of 1.5 percent.
b. A certificate of deposit with a fixed maturity date that can only be withdrawn by the owner serving written notice.
c. A demand deposit in which no withdrawal activity is recorded for three months.
d. A Foreign Currency Fixed Deposit (or FCFD).

6. The best description of risk management at a commercial bank is that:

a. a commercial bank manages risk by employing risk management executives who decide which loans and investments stand the best chance of earning profit.
b. a commercial bank manages risk by charging a higher rate of interest for loans than it pays out to depositors.
c. a commercial bank manages risk by using money from time deposits to invest in mutual funds, hedge funds, and sovereign funds.
d. a commercial bank forestalls loan and investment risk by maintaining an appropriate and regulated reserve ratio.

7. The interbank loan rate is set by the:

a. Federal Reserve Bank.
b. Securities and Exchange Commission.
c. state in which the bank is licensed.
d. FDIC.

8. The Treasury Department's Office of the Controller of the Currency is important because:

a. it licenses and regulates national banks to ensure that they meet Treasury reserve, insurance, and operational requirements.
b. it provides cash reserves to savings and loans in order to fund the purchase and sale of Treasury bills and bonds.
c. it sets the interbank loan rate.
d. it loans currency to member banks and S&Ls so that they make lending possible for small businesses.

9. Interbank loans at the federal funds rate are typically made when:

a. the interest rate on long-term home mortgages is higher than the federal funds rate.
b. a bank's reserve levels have fallen below federal reserve requirements to the degree that the bank needs to earn more profits to build them up again.
c. a bank builds up cash reserves in excess of the federal reserve requirements and gains additional revenues by lending it out.
d. a bank goes to the regional Federal Reserve Bank for a bailout.

10. One of the chief reasons that the Federal Reserve sets the federal funds rate lower than the rate for commercial lending is because:

a. Federal Reserve management wishes to stimulate lending for housing and other purposes while stabilizing the loan experience of commercial and individual borrowers.
b. the Federal Reserve wishes to stimulate the economy by making money available to borrowers.
c. a higher federal funds rate would slow the economy.
d. all of the above.

11. The advantage for a bank that is majority held by a "holding company" is that:

a. such banks are free to engage in "non-bank" activities like investment, financial management, and mortgage banking if such operations are deemed in the public interest.
b. such banks are largely unregulated in terms of market competition.
c. such banks concentrate on core activities like home loans, time deposits, and providing consumer savings and checking accounts.
d. all of the above.

12. The Federal Reserve adds to or contracts the money supply through:

a. the FDIC.
b. open market operations.
c. Fanny Mae and Freddie Mac.
d. encouragement of foreign investment.

13. The best example of the relationship between the discount rate and the money supply is seen in which of the following statements?

a. When the discount rate is raised, the money supply increases.
b. When the discount rate is raised, the money supply shrinks.
c. When the discount rate is lowered, the money supply shrinks.
d. When the discount rate is lowered, the money supply is unaffected.

14. The chief tools of the Federal Reserve's monetary controls are:

a. quantitative easing, issuance of paper currency, and inflation controls.
b. Treasury bonds, Treasury bills, and CDOs.
c. open market operations, the federal funds rate, the reserve ratio requirements, and the discount rate.
d. regulation of the securities industry, buying stocks and bonds of troubled financial institutions, and directing Treasury.

15. The statement that best defines the Federal Reserve's open market operations (OMO) is:

a. a public open meeting to decide what kind of statement to make in order to influence the economy.
b. a monetary control through which the Federal Reserve sets open market rates for government securities.
c. a monetary control by means of which the Federal Reserve injects money into the economy through the purchase or sale of government securities.
d. a meeting of the FOMC (Federal Open Market Committee) in which committee members, led by the Federal Reserve Chairman, set interest rates.

16. The FDIC provides deposit insurance:

a. to member banks that offer time deposits, checking and savings accounts, NOW accounts, life insurance accounts, and CDs.
b. to member banks that maintain checking and savings accounts, investment accounts, CDs, and money market accounts.
c. to member banks that offer NOW accounts, checking and savings accounts, and CDs and other time deposits, and that display a sign indicating FDIC insurance.
d. to member banks that offer NOW accounts, checking and savings accounts, CDs and other time deposits, and safe mutual funds that meet certain federal minimal risk requirements.

17. The structure of the FRS, or Federal Reserve System, consists of:

a. the Treasury Department, the Federal Reserve agency in New York, 12 regional Federal Reserve Banks, and the Federal Open Market Committee.
b. a central government agency in New York City, a Federal Reserve Chairman in Washington, D.C., and 12 regional Federal Reserve Banks.
c. the Treasury Department office in Washington, D.C., and 12 regional Federal Reserve Banks.
d. a central agency located in Washington, D.C., and 12 regional Federal Reserve Banks.

18. How could "quantitative easing" best be used as a tool of monetary policy during a recession?

a. Quantitative easing should be used when interest rates are in the range of three to five percent and GDP growth is recessionary.
b. Quantitative easing can be used to purchase mortgage-backed securities.
c. Quantitative easing can be used to inflate prices.
d. Quantitative easing should be used only when interest rates are close to zero and more stimulative measures are required to revive an economy.

19. The relationship between a foreign currency like the Chinese yuan and the US dollar can affect which of the following areas?

a. Supply chain efficiency.
b. Interest rates in both countries.
c. Worldwide price inflation.
d. Imports/exports.

20. The statement that best explains the dangers of "quantitative easing" is:

a. that it could discourage business borrowing and lending.
b. that it could leave too much money chasing too few goods, thereby causing price inflation.
c. that it could cause widespread unemployment.
d. that it could diminish productive capacity.

21. The difference between the GDP and the GNP is that:

a. GDP adds in the additional factor of foreign investment earnings after subtracting foreign investments in the US economy.
b. GNP adds in the additional factor of what Americans earned from foreign investment after subtracting what foreign residents earn from US investments.
c. GDP is the modern term for what used to be called GNP.
d. gross national product refers to the value of goods and services produced only in the continental US, whereas gross domestic product counts the foreign/domestic investment earnings factor.

22. Monetarist economists differ from Keynesians in that:

a. Keynesian economists place greater emphasis on strictly monetary controls than on government expenditures.
b. Keynesian economists believe that government spending has as great or a greater role in managing the economy than does the stricter monetary policy of the monetarists.
c. monetarists believe that price controls and other government interventions are the best way of managing the economy.
d. monetarists do not put as much emphasis on the money supply as do the Keynesians in the task of managing the economy.

23. The economic period of the 1970s was marked by:

a. marked successes for the adherents of Keynesian economics.
b. a growth period of low inflation, low interest rates, moderate government spending, and near full employment.
c. a recessionary period of high inflation, high interest rates, increased government spending, and increasing unemployment.
d. all of the above.

24. The definition that best describes the relationship between savings and disposable income is:

a. savings are defined as income after taxes; disposable income refers to income left over after expenditures have been subtracted.
b. savings are defined as disposable income after consumption expenses have been subtracted; disposable income refers to income the individual can control—meaning after-tax income.
c. that there is no difference between savings and disposable income.
d. disposable income = savings – taxes.

25. Define what is meant by the "velocity" of money.

a. The velocity of money is expressed by the equation: Velocity = T1 (transaction) divided by (GNP – GDP).
b. The velocity of money refers to the speed at which the Federal Reserve can increase the money supply through its monetary policies.
c. The velocity of money refers to the median measure of time a dollar takes to move from one transaction to the next.
d. The velocity of money measures the rapidity with which money is spent, represented as the median number of times a dollar is spent in a specific period of time.

26. The statement that best expresses the impact of measuring monetary aggregates in central bank policy is:

a. that in a time of scarce resources, sharp increases in money supply can be used to guide central bank policy moves toward limiting money supply growth by interest rate increases.
b. that comparisons of M0, M1, M2, and M3 can determine the velocity of money.
c. that a sharp increase in money supply is an indication of inflation that must be controlled by interest rate manipulation.
d. that a sharp decrease in the money supply is an indication of inflation that must be controlled by interest rate manipulation.

27. When calculating money supply aggregates, M0 (M-zero) refers to:

a. physical cash and coin plus demand deposits and traveler's checks.
b. M2 minus M1.
c. hard currency, meaning physical cash and coin.
d. hard currency plus checking and savings accounts.

28. The component of the money aggregate that includes all of M1 plus savings deposits and money market shares is:

a. M0 (M-zero).
b. M2.
c. M3.
d. M1.

29. The currency termed the "euro" is controlled by:

a. the European Central Bank and a Governing Council made up of key members of the European Treasury Department.
b. the Euro zone Governing Council, made up of representatives of the 12 member countries, and a Treasury.
c. a Euro Treasury Department, the European Central Bank, and a Governing Council consisting of three permanent members.
d. the European Central Bank and a Governing Council made up from representatives of each of the 16 Euro zone members.

30. The statement that best demonstrates the concept of interest rate parity in foreign exchange markets is:

a. that interest rate differences between two countries have an inverse relationship to the difference in forward exchange rates and the spot exchange rate in both countries.
b. that a rise in spot interest rates in a trading partner country directly correlates to a rise in spot interest rates in the other partner country.
c. that a rise in spot interest rates in one trading partner country directly correlates to a drop in spot interest rates in the other trading partner country.
d. that interest rate differences between two countries correlate directly to the difference in forward exchange rates and the spot exchange rate.

31. The post-WWII GATT treaty was replaced in 1995 by:

a. forex.
b. the G-20 Nations Agreements.
c. NAFTA.
d. the WTO.

32. Two prominent categories of a country's balance of payments are:

a. current accounts and capital accounts.
b. government and corporate investment in foreign countries.
c. international bank deposits and investments in foreign business.
d. imports and exports.

33. The statement that best exemplifies economic behavior using the liquidity preference theory is:

a. people will put their money into cash or bonds, depending on the amount of fear or confidence they have in the economy.
b. people will put their money into cash or bonds randomly and regardless of the direction of interest rates.
c. people will choose to put their money in cash or invest it in bonds, depending on whether they believe interest rates will rise or fall.
d. people who expect interest rates to rise will use their cash to buy bonds.

34. The difference between the CPI and the PPI is:

a. the CPI represents retail prices whereas the PPI represents cheaper wholesale prices based on the cost of producing goods.
b. the CPI measures an index of prices paid to the producers of a good whereas the PPI measures what the consumer actually paid for the goods.
c. the CPI factors in retail discounts whereas the PPI measures the cost of producing goods.
d. the CPI measures an index of prices from the consumer standpoint, whereas the PPI measures it from the producer point of view.

35. The statement that best explains the functioning of the Federal Reserve's discount window is:

a. eligible financial institutions with liquidity issues are permitted to borrow money directly from the Federal Reserve at the prime rate.
b. eligible financial institutions are permitted to borrow directly from the Federal Reserve at the discount rate to resolve short-term crises of liquidity if they are on a sound financial footing.
c. eligible financial institutions are permitted to borrow money at the Federal Reserve's repo rate to resolve short-term crises of liquidity.
d. eligible financial institutions are permitted to make interbank overnight loans at the federal funds rate.

36. The language used after meetings of the Federal Reserve's Federal Open Market Committee can affect financial markets because:

a. financial analysts anxiously await the language of the FOMC announcements as a gauge as to the direction and stability of interest rates.
b. the "announcement effect" of Federal Reserve public comments following FOMC decisions about rates causes markets to move up, down, or sideways.
c. The language of public comments following FOMC meetings is highly stylized, cautious, and sensitive to financial market conditions because misinterpretation can have negative effects for an economy.
d. all of the above.

37. In reference to the Federal Reserve's open market operations, the so-called "multiplier effect" means:

a. that the Fed buys securities on the open market and, through a process called "double counting," multiplies the amount of its cash reserve.
b. that the Fed buys securities on the open market and, through returns on its investments, increases the money supply.
c. that the Fed buys securities on the open market, provides cash to the institution that sold the securities, and, through the loan and investment process that ensues, the bank possesses both a loan asset and a bank deposit at the same time.
d. all of the above.

38. The Federal Reserve Bank examiners monitor bank and holding company activities in order to:

a. obtain detailed information on the financial institution's accounts and practices to ensure that it is not engaged in risky lending practices.
b. ensure that consumers are not subject to predatory lending practices.
c. review the institution's assets and liabilities, and pay particular attention to the soundness of the bank's investments and adherence to law and ethical practice.
d. all of the above.

39. Describe the manner in which new money enters the cash stream.

a. The Federal Reserve Bank controls the currency, directing the Bureau of Engraving and Printing to print paper money and the US Mint to make coinage, and then moves the money to the regional central banks, which make it available to commercial banks.
b. The Treasury Department prints paper money and mints coins, the amount of which is tallied at the Federal Reserve, before it is released to commercial banks.
c. The Federal Reserve Bank prints paper money and mints coins, and loans the funds to commercial banks.
d. Regional central banks determine the amount of money needed in the district and the Federal Reserve accommodates the request by directing the Treasury to print money and the US Mint to mint coinage.

40. The difference between monetary policy and fiscal policy is:

a. that monetary policy relies on such tools as tax increases, tax cuts, and increased government spending, while fiscal policy depends on using tools of interest rate manipulation to achieve desired economic changes.
b. that monetary policy is set by a governing body, whereas fiscal policy refers to the tools used by a central bank to manipulate the economy.
c. that monetary policy is set by a central bank, whereas fiscal policy derives from a national government's economic policy.
d. that monetary policy is set by the US Treasury Department, while fiscal policy is set by the Federal Reserve.

41. In the wake of the September 2008 US economic crisis, a prominent investment bank converted itself from an investment bank to a bank holding company with the regulatory result that:

a. the Treasury Department became chief regulator of its activities.
b. the Securities and Exchange Commission became the chief regulator of its activities.
c. the Federal Reserve became the chief regulator of its activities.
d. the US Congress became the temporary chief regulator of its activities.

42. The research and analysis branch of an investment firm issues excessively optimistic performance reports that it shares with the public and with their investment banking colleagues.

a. There is nothing wrong with issuing overly optimistic reports to investment banking colleagues as long as the same information is shared with the public.
b. The overly optimistic reports are an important and legitimate way of increasing an investment firm's business.
c. Since large and small public investors, as well as investment bankers, would benefit from optimistic financial performance reports, there is no conflict of interest.
d. The SEC may be interested in such a case because financial reports must not be biased toward the profit motives of investment banks.

43. An increase in the cost of goods and services would:

a. not change the demand for money.
b. increase the demand for money.
c. decrease the demand for money.
d. decrease the money supply.

44. Supply-side economists believe:

a. that an unfettered market of investors, manufacturers, producers of goods and services, and job creators, combined with tax cuts, will stimulate the economy for everyone.
b. economic advantages are derived from government spending on infrastructure programs, lower taxation, and a minimal regulatory environment.
c. the government can create jobs and keep unemployment rates in an acceptable range by expanding government agencies and subsidizing aggregate demand.
d. all of the above.

45. A general definition of the "Laffer Curve" is that it:

a. is a classic x,y graph demonstrating that a gradually rising tax curve does not negatively affect productivity because graduated taxes are perceived as being fair.
b. proves that productivity is neither affected nor linked to taxation.
c. is a classic x,y graph showing that tax revenues rise consistent with tax increases until a certain point of taxation is reached, whereupon productivity declines.
d. illustrates that tax increases mean that more revenues flow to government so that it can better provide services to American citizens.

46. The international agency that was formed pursuant to the Bretton Woods agreement and for the stability of international trade is:

a. the General Agreement on Tariffs and Trade.
b. the International Monetary Fund.
c. the World Trade Organization.
d. the North American Free Trade Agreement.

47. Aside from fiscal and monetary tools, the national economy is subject to "automatic stabilizers." Define "automatic stabilizers."

a. Automatic stabilizers are economic mechanisms that try to prevent wild swings in the economy. Examples include unemployment insurance, food stamps, Social Security benefits, and other in-place entitlement programs.
b. Automatic stabilizers are tax and interest rate mechanisms that can be immediately implemented by government economists to stabilize the economy.
c. Automatic stabilizers refer to the ability of the Federal Reserve and the US Treasury to manage the economy in times of severe economic crisis such as occurred in September 2008.
d. All of the above.

48. Which of the following is an example of how federal deficits and borrowing from other countries may have an impact on trade policies?

a. China's purchase of US debt has decreased Chinese exports to the US
b. The Greek government is threatened by deficits caused by excessive spending on social programs and must now borrow from the United States.
c. China has purchased a large amount of US debt even while it is involved in trade and currency disputes with the US, a relationship that could give it an advantage in trade and policy disputes.
d. All of the suggested answers are examples of the manner in which growing deficits can affect trade.

49. All of the conditions noted below may result from a national debt that is increasing in relationship to gross domestic product EXCEPT:

a. a lack of confidence in the economy.
b. increased spending by private industry.
c. a weakening of the currency.
d. diminished investment and savings.

50. Which of the followings statements is FALSE?

a. A trade deficit occurs when the balance of trade reflects more credit items than it does debit items.
b. A trade deficit negatively affects a country's economy when it occurs during a recession, whereas it tends to correct itself in an expansionary period of the economy.
c. Balance of trade credit items include foreign investment, exports, and foreign spending in the domestic economy.
d. Balance of Trade debit items include imports, foreign aid, overseas domestic spending, and overseas investment.

Answer Key and Explanations

1. D: All of the answers apply to the concept of money, but none of the characteristics would have meaning if the commodity being used as money is not widely accepted in trade. Native Americans often used seashells, beads, and a variety of things known as "wampum." It's acceptance in trade was what made it count as money. Fungibility refers to the ease with which money can flow from one party or place to another. Though it was accepted currency during historical times, wampum was less fungible than gold coins. For example, gold coins were more easily transportable and easier to handle as they passed from hand to hand.

2. C: Answer "c" is FALSE and is also the correct answer because there is no longer any "gold standard," nor any "silver standard." A dollar cannot be exchanged for a specific amount of silver or gold. The one thing that characterizes "fiat money" is that it can't be redeemed for anything—not for gold or silver, nor for any other commodity. Fiat money is "declared" by a government to have meaning and value. The value is derived from the strength of the government's economy. The use of this type of specie (fiat money) allows a government banking system to put more or less of it in circulation, as part of its "monetary policy." Regulating the money supply is one way of making adjustments to economic conditions. Answer choices "a," "b," and "d" are all true.

3. B: Money that is intrinsically worthless but backed up by a valuable substance is called representative money. A certificate is made of paper, but it's not money unless it can be exchanged for something. "D" would therefore be an incorrect answer. But if a certificate guarantees exchange of a specific amount of silver or other valuable metal, it is "representative money." Commodity money is of a type that trades of itself; commodity money can consist of any scarce commodity that is deemed to have value—jewels, precious metals, even glass beads. Fiat money, on the other hand, has no intrinsic value, but is rather a promise of value. The US dollar and the euro are examples of fiat money.

4. A: The other answer choices are nonsensical or irrelevant. The use of money as a "unit of account" is a way of measuring the value of ownership items like houses, cars, clothing, and food, and also a means of valuing the cost of operations and capital holdings. Since a dollar has relatively stable value, the number of dollars used to buy something serves as a comparative measurement. One car may have a sticker price of $26,000, while another has a price tag of $34,000. As such, the dollar is a unit of account used by the holder in comparing values. It is the same with clothing, wages, factories, savings deposits, or just about anything. Money is the "unit of account" by which goods, wages, and a variety of other things can be measured.

5. C: Answer choice "c" is not a time deposit, whether there is activity on the account or not. Therefore, answer "c" is the correct answer. CDs, or certificates of deposit, are time deposits. Time requirements for time deposit CDs are for a minimum of one month but may extend into years. Time deposits guarantee a specified rate of interest with the requirement that the deposits remain on account for a period of time (the maturity date) without withdrawal. Early withdrawal subjects the account to penalties. A person may establish a Foreign Currency Fixed Deposit (FCFD) account under similar terms. FCFDs contain currency risk, since dollars must first be converted into the host currency and then changed back to dollars at the end of the term.

6. D: Banking regulations require that commercial banks maintain proper reserve ratios that can keep the bank afloat during "bank runs," a high incidence of default, or other crises. Charging a higher rate of interest for loans than it pays for time deposits helps a commercial bank only if loans never default. That's not realistic, as the current recession/crisis shows. Investing in "funds" helps a bank's profit and bottom line. but investment firms sometimes go bankrupt, too. Commercial banking chains do employ risk managers who can set policies, but policies often come up short of expectations, especially during economic crises.

7. A: Another name for the interbank loan rate is the federal funds rate. Knowing that, you would likely have selected the correct answer choice of "a," the Federal Reserve Bank. The FDIC, or Federal Deposit Insurance Corporation, insures bank deposits. The SEC regulates security trades. States do set some banking regulations, but they do not set interest rates for interbank loans. In fact, setting the federal funds rate for interbank loans is one of the most important and primary functions of the Federal Reserve System.

8. A: In addition to national bank licensing, the Office of the Controller of Currency (OCC) ensures that banks are meeting reserve requirements and that they become members of the FDIC. The Office of the Controller of Currency also investigates potential criminal money-laundering activities and cases of possible terrorist funding. You probably remember that the Federal Reserve sets the interest rate for interbank loans, so you can rule out choice "c." Choice "d" is also incorrect and makes little sense. If you knew that answer option was incorrect, you probably wouldn't choose "b" either.

9. C: The Federal Reserve Bank sets the federal funds rate and the reserve requirements for banks. If a bank holds reserves in excess of the federal requirement, it may earn additional profits by loaning that money out for additional profit with dwindling reserves at the federal funds rate of interest. Choice "d" is wrong because it should never be necessary for the Federal Reserve to "bail out" a bank. Nor does answer choice "a" make sense, because the federal funds rate is lower than the housing mortgage rate precisely to stimulate housing, so that condition is always the case. Answer "b" has it exactly backwards. If a bank doesn't have enough cash reserves to meet obligations, the federal reserve requirements restrict more lending.

10. D: One means of stimulating or slowing the economy is by controlling interest rates. A lower federal funds rate spreads money around to institutions with dwindling reserves and, therefore, more money is available for borrowing. Lower federal funds rates translate to lower interest rates for consumers and other borrowers. If the availability of money causes a rapid rise in prices, the Federal Reserve may slow down borrowing by a marginal increase in the federal funds rate. The ideal objective is always economic stability—stable financial institutions, steady growth, and a low inflation rate.

11. A: Banks that are owned by holding companies may be allowed by regulators to expand their activities into investment, financial management, insurance, and other businesses. They do not concentrate on limited "thrift" activities like the consumer lending mentioned in answer choice "c." Answer choice "b" would be incorrect because banking is a heavily regulated industry. Answer choice "b" is often argued but, in fact, banking regulations are designed so that one competitor does not become so large and dominant as to drive out smaller competitors.

12. B: The question asks how the "Federal Reserve" manipulates the money supply. It does so through choice "b," open market operations. The FDIC refers to the Federal Deposit Insurance Corporation. Essentially, this government agency insures consumer savings to the current maximum limit of $250,000 (previously $100,000), but only in FDIC-insured banks. This is important, but it has no effect on for the money supply. On the other hand, Fannie Mae and Freddie Mac help to make money available for home lending, but this is not a big mover of the money supply. Foreign investment does contribute to the US economy, but this involves currency exchange rather than money supply.

13. B: Raising the interest rate banks must pay when borrowing from the Fed can discourage borrowing, resulting in a decrease in money supply, so "b" is the correct answer. The discount rate refers to the interest rate charged when banks borrow money from the Federal Reserve banking system. The interest rate fluctuates either through defensive maneuvers or in response to cyclical spending habits. The use of the discount rate is just one tool of Federal Reserve monetary policy, but it is often effective, so answer "d" is incorrect. A lowered discount rate can encourage borrowing, putting more money in circulation, and increasing the money supply. Therefore, answer choice "c" is incorrect.

14. C: The key concept in considering "monetary controls" is the word "control." Most of the answer options are vague and incidental to the idea of monetary controls. The SEC regulates the securities industry and the Treasury is independent, so answer "d" is clearly wrong. Moreover, bailouts constitute very unusual activity for the Federal Reserve. On the other hand, the Federal Reserve has the direct authority to set the federal funds rate and the discount rate. It makes decisions regarding raising or lowering rates at meetings of the FOMC. The Fed can also alter bank reserve ratio requirements. These are direct tools that can stimulate or slow down economic activity, depending on the goal.

15. C: Meetings of the Federal Open Market Committee attract a lot of attention from financial analysts because they signal the direction of interest rates, as suggested by answer "d." This is not what is meant by "open market operations," however. The actual "open market operations" of the Federal Reserve involve buying and selling government securities with the intent of adding or removing money from the US banking system. When the Fed buys government securities, it stimulates economic growth because it adds money to the banking system. Similarly, it may slow growth, usually with the intent of controlling inflation, by selling government securities and thus removing money from the banking system.

16. C: To answer the question correctly, you have to know what types of financial holdings cannot be insured by the FDIC. Of course, only member banks can be insured, since membership contributes to the costs of operation of the FDIC. Each of the incorrect answer choices contains one type of financial vehicle that is not covered by FDIC insurance. Life insurance, investment accounts, and mutual fund accounts of any type are not covered by FDIC insurance, regardless of risk factors.

17. C: The entire Federal Reserve banking system, sometimes called the "Central Bank" of the United States, consists of a central government agency in Washington, D.C., and 12 regional member banks located in large cities: San Francisco, Minneapolis, Chicago, Kansas City, Dallas, St. Louis, Cleveland, Atlanta, Richmond, Philadelphia, New York, and Boston. The mention of the "Treasury" rules those answers out because the Treasury Department is intended to be separate from the FRS. Another difference is that "Treasury" has a cabinet-level position—Secretary of the Treasury. Choice "b" is incorrect because, though the New York Fed is important because of its location, it is not the "headquarters" of the FRS, which is a government agency located in Washington, D.C.

18. D: It would be of help in answering this question to know what quantitative easing is. Quantitative easing refers to the practice of the Federal Reserve of buying government and other securities in the open market. The result is to flood the economy with money that is available for use by finance, industry, and other consumers. Quantitative easing should be used only when interest rate stimulation has put rates close to zero and further economic stimulation is needed.

19. D: The correct answer is that currency differences between trading partners have a direct influence on imports and exports, as noted in option "d." If the US dollar is especially strong against the yuan, it would encourage US import of Chinese goods and make Chinese import of American goods expensive. Many economists and business leaders believe that this is the case right now, and that China should appreciate (increase the value of) its currency, the yuan, in the interest of fair trade. The Chinese respond that Chinese industries operate with a 3 percent profit margin and that a 1 percent increase in the yuan's value would subject their industries to risk of failure.

20. B: Keep in mind that quantitative easing should be generally employed by the central bank during recessionary periods when the federal funds rate, discount rate, and other interest rates are already unusually low. When interest rate controls have not sufficiently stimulated the economy, quantitative easing can be used to flood the economy with additional available cash that can be used to produce, hire, lend, or borrow, or for whatever purposes the economy demands. There is a danger, however, that output can slow so much that there is too much money chasing too few goods. This condition results in price inflation.

21. B: Clear definitions of GDP and GNP would be helpful in answering this question. GNP can be confusing because it means gross national product and this could lead some people to think it was limited to the continental US In fact, the opposite is true. GNP encompasses the full gross domestic product but adds in an extra factor, which is what the US earns from foreign investments after subtracting what foreign investors earn from US investments.

22. B: The Keynesians believe that government spending can benefit the economy during times of unemployment and other crises. The policies of the "monetarists" place more emphasis on money supply manipulation through such tools as the discount rate and the federal funds rate. Monetarists do not believe that creating government jobs and making other government expenditures are the best way to stimulate the economy. Answer choice "d" has it just the opposite of the way it really is.

23. C: You should have ruled out "d" right way because "b" and "c" are directly contradictory. Then the question becomes one of determining whether or not the 1970s were a period of marked successes for the Keynesians. The US had increased government spending because of the Vietnam War and the Great Society expenditures. Government spending infused cash into the economy so that interest rates on savings rose to unprecedented highs. Unemployment increased as the US entered a long recessionary period.

24. B: The reason for the difference is that a person or business entity has control over disposable income. Disposable income is the amount left over after taxes (which a person cannot much control). Disposable income may be applied to savings or it may be entirely spent on necessary and unnecessary expenses. "C" and "d" are wrong because the formula supplied is incorrect and because there is a difference between the two terms. Keeping the idea of "control" in mind should help you to differentiate these terms and lead you to the correct answer choice.

25. D: The velocity of money is the frequency and rapidity with which people spend money. The velocity of money is often expressed as the median number of times a dollar is spent in a specific period of time. The velocity of money is calculated as $V = (P \times Q)/M$, in which P is the price level, Q is nominal GDP, and M is money supply. A sharp increase in the velocity of money is thought to be a cause of inflation.

26. A: Answers "c" and "d" express a very narrow and inaccurate viewpoint, in that sharp increases or sharp decreases are not, by themselves, indicative of inflation. Similarly, answer choice "b" limits the perspective to the velocity of money, which, in itself, is not of much use in determining the central bank's monetary policy. The purpose of money supply measurement is to determine whether there is precipitous money supply growth (M0, M1, M2, and to a lesser extent M3) at a time when resources are scarce, a situation in which too much money may be chasing too few goods. This is textbook inflation.

27. C: M0 is the basic fundamental money with which we are all familiar, the type you can hold in your hands. The other two important components of money supply are M1 and M2. M3 hasn't been measured for use by the Federal Reserve since 2006, though some financial analysts find it a useful figure. Of course, the purpose of measuring the money aggregate is because of its correlation to inflation, GDP, and unemployment. Some analysts believe that the relationship between money supply and Fed action on the discount and federal funds rates is tenuous.

28. B: M0 (M-zero) refers to all hard currency and cash. M1 consists of all physical currency plus demand deposits and traveler's checks. M2 consists of all of M1 plus both savings deposits and money market shares. M3 (no longer used by the Fed in its calculations) consists of M0, M1, and M2, and adds in large institutional funds and "jumbo" time deposits greater than $100,000.

29. D: The Euro zone system has been largely successful, though it has been criticized because it cannot have and does not have a common Treasury. Because of this, those answer options that mention a Euro "Treasury" are incorrect. In fact, the euro is supported by the European Central Bank and its governing body, the European Central Bank Governing Council. The Governing Council is made up of 16 members (not 12), one from each member nation. One of the problems faced by the European Central Bank is the disparate economic conditions and spending in various member nations. For example, the current pressing fiscal crisis in Greece poses a threat to the euro's stability.

30. D: The idea behind interest rate parity is that differences in forward and spot exchange rates in trading partner countries directly relate to interest rate differences in the two countries. This drive toward interest rate parity causes foreign exchange rates to fluctuate and generates a considerable amount of currency speculation or arbitrage—the profit gained by currencies with temporary fractional fluctuating values in different countries. Of course, arbitrage can occur with the value of assets other than currency assets.

31. D: The 1947 GATT treaty (General Agreement on Tariffs and Trade) was designed to help weakened nations recover from the economic devastation of WWII. GATT was aimed at tariffs and quotas that restricted trade between stronger and weaker countries, and it also intervened with government subsidies that stultified competition and open markets. The WTO has the same goals as GATT. International trade is also expedited by meetings, discussions, and agreements between the G-20 countries, formed from the finance ministers and central bankers of 19 large countries plus the EU. NAFTA is a limited trade agreement between the US, Canada, and Mexico only.

32. A: Current account balances consist of interest payments, overseas profits, tourism, and the import/export ratio. Capital accounts consist of international bank deposits, investment, and debt securities. The balance of payments is important because it affects currency values. When there is a payment deficit in one country, the currency depreciates and results in a decrease in confidence in the country's economic strength. Countries that find themselves in this situation may decide to export precious metals like gold or use stronger currencies to settle their debts.

33. C: The liquidity preference theory was a favorite of the economist John Maynard Keynes. Keynes' model of the liquidity preference theory held that people who perceived rising interest rates will choose to maintain the liquidity of cash. On the other hand, people who watched declining interest rates tended to put their cash into bonds. Adherents of this theory believe that the velocity of money was an important factor regarding where they kept their money; the theory holds that the velocity of money would rise or fall consistent with interest rates.

34. D: The CPI, or consumer price index, measures a basket or index of consumer goods in terms of what the consumer actually paid for them. The PPI, or producer price index, measures the prices that are received by the producer or manufacturer of a good. PPI focuses on industry-produced goods, commodity-produced goods, and items in various stages of production. CPI entails measuring the most important goods and services, such as consumer goods, food, transportation, and medical services. The CPI is an average, with the goods or services weighted according to their importance to the consumer.

35. B: Financial institutions are permitted to borrow directly from the Federal Reserve at the discount rate if they are on a sound financial footing. Usually the reason for doing so is to resolve short-term liquidity problems and so that they can maintain appropriate reserve ratios. The Fed's discount window is open only to institutions that are on a reliable and sound financial footing. When such lending occurred originally, the discount window was used only in times of emergency and when other sources of capital were unavailable. In recent times, that restraint has eased and the discount window is used routinely. There was much use of the Federal Reserve discount window to address the US economic crisis of 2008-2009.

35. D: The FOMC of the Federal Reserve Bank meets periodically to determine what tools or postures must be held with respect to the general economy. In an effective Federal Reserve, statements made after the meetings will signal long-term moves in interest rates. Should the Federal Reserve announcements come as a surprise, financial markets may be thrown into turmoil. A precipitous announced increase or decrease in interest rates will cause financial investors to re-shuffle their investment strategies. The language used in Federal Reserve announcements must always be careful and well thought out.

37. C: When the Federal Reserve purchases securities from commercial banks and thrift institutions, it is in effect increasing the monetary base. This makes sense, since the money used to purchase the securities goes into bank reserves, which then can be lent to individuals and businesses. Some of the loaned money will be invested back in the bank. At this point, the money will exist in the banking system twice: both as an outstanding loan that the bank considers an asset, and as a bank deposit that the bank can use to make investments of its own.

38. D: In monitoring banks and holding companies, the Federal Reserve Bank examiners are directed to perform all the noted functions. In the current and ongoing crisis, it seems that "systemic failure" was perhaps human failure. Risky lending practices, predatory lending, ethical breaches, and insufficient reserves contributed to the economic collapse of late 2008. This economic cataclysm led to unprecedented action by the Federal Reserve to buttress financial institutions by all means available—near-zero interest rates, cash infusions, so-called bailouts, open market operations, and a variety of newly contrived tools.

39. A: The Federal Reserve controls the money supply, directing the Bureau of Engraving and Printing to print it and the US mint to coin it. Both the Bureau of Engraving and Printing and the US Mint are agencies within the US Department of the Treasury. The money then goes to the 12 central banks that make it available by loans to commercial banks. From there, it goes into public circulation in the form of loans, cashed checks, et cetera. Printed money generally lasts about three years in circulation; bills of larger denomination last longer, as they generally receive a lesser amount of handling.

40. C: Monetary policy is strictly within the aegis of the Federal Reserve System. Monetary policy refers to the authority of the Federal Reserve to set key interest rates like the federal funds rate and the discount rate, both of which can slow or stimulate growth in the economy. On the other hand, fiscal policy refers to the authority of a government to increase taxes, cut taxes, and set policies that change economic conditions. A legislated tax cut, for example, gives businesses additional capital that can be saved, reinvested, or used to expand or hire additional workers.

41. C: Answer option "c" is correct because the SEC has been the traditional regulator and overseer of investment banks. When investment banks like Goldman Sachs became holding companies with bank ownership, they fell under the regulatory mantle of the Federal Reserve, but also acquired the advantages of being able to receive loans from the Fed. It's a matter of authorities. The US Congress, mentioned in answer "d," has the authority to investigate and legislate, but not to directly regulate.

42. D: Although the determination that a financial report is overly optimistic or issued with the intent of increasing a firm's business is a matter of degree, sometimes decided in federal courts. But the SEC has the obligation to ensure that outside investors do not become victims of insider trading activities or conflicts of interest. Failing to protect investor interests could result in judicial penalties for the SEC itself. The SEC set its own precedent in a 2003 case in which it sued various Wall Street investment firms for issuing overly optimistic stock research in order to win business for their investment arms.

43. B: "B" is the best answer because a greater demand for money naturally follows increases in the costs of goods and services. Consumers react to higher prices by an increased need to withdraw money to pay for daily living expenses and other necessary goods and services. The demand for money becomes even more pronounced in businesses that require a larger amount of operational capital. In addition, the increased price of raw materials in manufacturing will cause producers to raise their own prices, exacerbating demand for cash.

44. A: "A" is the correct answer, but, except for spending on infrastructure, "b" would be right, too. The problem with answer "b" is that supply-side economists do not believe that government-created infrastructure jobs are permanent and that they may lead to additional restrictive tax burdens. Option "c" more aptly describes demand-side economists. Supply-side economists point to budget deficits, government borrowing, and unneeded spending for inflation and dollar devaluation. Supply-siders believe that by reducing taxes and regulation, government will encourage business investment and production, and expedite job creation.

45. C: The Laffer curve is a classic x,y graph showing that tax revenues rise consistent with tax increases until a certain point of taxation is reached, whereupon productivity declines. One interesting thing about the Laffer curve is that it doesn't mention productivity, but has tax increases and tax revenues on its x and y axes. The assumption is that tax revenues decline after reaching a certain point of high taxation. The extreme of the view is that 100 percent taxation would result in no reason to work for taxable wages because there would be no incentive or reason to do so.

45. B: The IMF, or International Monetary Fund, was established in the wake of the Bretton Woods agreement, which established stable and consistent monetary values to enable trade between nations. Originally, international currencies were pegged to gold but many currencies, including the dollar, were "floated" in the early 1970s. The IMF facilitates the expansion of trade by loaning money to member countries and resolving trade imbalances.

47. A: A distinction must be made between "tools" and "stabilizers." Setting the federal funds rate or the discount rate are tools of the Federal Reserve. Raising taxes or passing tax cuts are fiscal policies that can be used by national and state policies to stimulate or restrain the economy. On the other hand, "automatic" stabilizers are embedded in the economy through entitlements, that is, social benefits that were intended to protect people against violent downturns like the Great Depression and also the current unemployment and jobs crisis. Another name for "automatic stabilizers" is "transfer payments."

48. C: In order to eliminate "d," you can look for a single error in "all of the above." The error in "a," for example, is that Chinese purchase of US debt has had the opposite effect, as the US debt purchases shore up the dollar against the dollar-pegged yuan. This makes Chinese goods cheaper, increasing Chinese exports to the US Answer choice "b" is not a good answer because the Greek government is supported by the European Union and would be "backstopped" from member countries.

49. B: Increased national debts typically come from government overspending, which tends to crowd out spending from the private sector through job creation and other effects. Along the same lines, savings and investment are diminished. An increasing national debt also may trigger a lack of confidence in the economy and consumers may react negatively, triggering further contractions. The national debt is relational rather than just a number. What seems to be a very large national debt for a country with low output may be entirely manageable if output in the form of GDP is high in proportion to the debt.

50. A: The statement in "a" would be correct if it read: "A trade deficit occurs when the balance of trade reflects more DEBIT items than it does CREDIT items." The other statements are all true. Answer options "c" and "d" indicate what credit and debits are counted when measuring balance of trade (BOT). It should be noted that a trade deficit is not in itself destructive to an economy, as trade deficits tend to right themselves in a healthy, expanding economy. The real danger of a trade deficit occurs when an economy is in contraction or recession. In recessionary times, governments wish to stimulate production and other economic activity by exporting products and services to foreign markets. Exporting more is one way to do that.

How to Overcome Test Anxiety

Just the thought of taking a test is enough to make most people a little nervous. A test is an important event that can have a long-term impact on your future, so it's important to take it seriously and it's natural to feel anxious about performing well. But just because anxiety is normal, that doesn't mean that it's helpful in test taking, or that you should simply accept it as part of your life. Anxiety can have a variety of effects. These effects can be mild, like making you feel slightly nervous, or severe, like blocking your ability to focus or remember even a simple detail.

If you experience test anxiety—whether severe or mild—it's important to know how to beat it. To discover this, first you need to understand what causes test anxiety.

Causes of Test Anxiety

While we often think of anxiety as an uncontrollable emotional state, it can actually be caused by simple, practical things. One of the most common causes of test anxiety is that a person does not feel adequately prepared for their test. This feeling can be the result of many different issues such as poor study habits or lack of organization, but the most common culprit is time management. Starting to study too late, failing to organize your study time to cover all of the material, or being distracted while you study will mean that you're not well prepared for the test. This may lead to cramming the night before, which will cause you to be physically and mentally exhausted for the test. Poor time management also contributes to feelings of stress, fear, and hopelessness as you realize you are not well prepared but don't know what to do about it.

Other times, test anxiety is not related to your preparation for the test but comes from unresolved fear. This may be a past failure on a test, or poor performance on tests in general. It may come from comparing yourself to others who seem to be performing better or from the stress of living up to expectations. Anxiety may be driven by fears of the future—how failure on this test would affect your educational and career goals. These fears are often completely irrational, but they can still negatively impact your test performance.

Elements of Test Anxiety

As mentioned earlier, test anxiety is considered to be an emotional state, but it has physical and mental components as well. Sometimes you may not even realize that you are suffering from test anxiety until you notice the physical symptoms. These can include trembling hands, rapid heartbeat, sweating, nausea, and tense muscles. Extreme anxiety may lead to fainting or vomiting. Obviously, any of these symptoms can have a negative impact on testing. It is important to recognize them as soon as they begin to occur so that you can address the problem before it damages your performance.

The mental components of test anxiety include trouble focusing and inability to remember learned information. During a test, your mind is on high alert, which can help you recall information and stay focused for an extended period of time. However, anxiety interferes with your mind's natural processes, causing you to blank out, even on the questions you know well. The strain of testing during anxiety makes it difficult to stay focused, especially on a test that may take several hours. Extreme anxiety can take a huge mental toll, making it difficult not only to recall test information but even to understand the test questions or pull your thoughts together.

Effects of Test Anxiety

Test anxiety is like a disease—if left untreated, it will get progressively worse. Anxiety leads to poor performance, and this reinforces the feelings of fear and failure, which in turn lead to poor performances on subsequent tests. It can grow from a mild nervousness to a crippling condition. If allowed to progress, test anxiety can have a big impact on your schooling, and consequently on your future.

Test anxiety can spread to other parts of your life. Anxiety on tests can become anxiety in any stressful situation, and blanking on a test can turn into panicking in a job situation. But fortunately, you don't have to let anxiety rule your testing and determine your grades. There are a number of relatively simple steps you can take to move past anxiety and function normally on a test and in the rest of life.

Physical Steps for Beating Test Anxiety

While test anxiety is a serious problem, the good news is that it can be overcome. It doesn't have to control your ability to think and remember information. While it may take time, you can begin taking steps today to beat anxiety.

Just as your first hint that you may be struggling with anxiety comes from the physical symptoms, the first step to treating it is also physical. Rest is crucial for having a clear, strong mind. If you are tired, it is much easier to give in to anxiety. But if you establish good sleep habits, your body and mind will be ready to perform optimally, without the strain of exhaustion. Additionally, sleeping well helps you to retain information better, so you're more likely to recall the answers when you see the test questions.

Getting good sleep means more than going to bed on time. It's important to allow your brain time to relax. Take study breaks from time to time so it doesn't get overworked, and don't study right before bed. Take time to rest your mind before trying to rest your body, or you may find it difficult to fall asleep.

Along with sleep, other aspects of physical health are important in preparing for a test. Good nutrition is vital for good brain function. Sugary foods and drinks may give a burst of energy but this burst is followed by a crash, both physically and emotionally. Instead, fuel your body with protein and vitamin-rich foods.

Also, drink plenty of water. Dehydration can lead to headaches and exhaustion, especially if your brain is already under stress from the rigors of the test. Particularly if your test is a long one, drink water during the breaks. And if possible, take an energy-boosting snack to eat between sections.

Along with sleep and diet, a third important part of physical health is exercise. Maintaining a steady workout schedule is helpful, but even taking 5-minute study breaks to walk can help get your blood pumping faster and clear your head. Exercise also releases endorphins, which contribute to a positive feeling and can help combat test anxiety.

When you nurture your physical health, you are also contributing to your mental health. If your body is healthy, your mind is much more likely to be healthy as well. So take time to rest, nourish your body with healthy food and water, and get moving as much as possible. Taking these physical steps will make you stronger and more able to take the mental steps necessary to overcome test anxiety.

Mental Steps for Beating Test Anxiety

Working on the mental side of test anxiety can be more challenging, but as with the physical side, there are clear steps you can take to overcome it. As mentioned earlier, test anxiety often stems from lack of preparation, so the obvious solution is to prepare for the test. Effective studying may be the most important weapon you have for beating test anxiety, but you can and should employ several other mental tools to combat fear.

First, boost your confidence by reminding yourself of past success—tests or projects that you aced. If you're putting as much effort into preparing for this test as you did for those, there's no reason you should expect to fail here. Work hard to prepare; then trust your preparation.

Second, surround yourself with encouraging people. It can be helpful to find a study group, but be sure that the people you're around will encourage a positive attitude. If you spend time with others who are anxious or cynical, this will only contribute to your own anxiety. Look for others who are motivated to study hard from a desire to succeed, not from a fear of failure.

Third, reward yourself. A test is physically and mentally tiring, even without anxiety, and it can be helpful to have something to look forward to. Plan an activity following the test, regardless of the outcome, such as going to a movie or getting ice cream.

When you are taking the test, if you find yourself beginning to feel anxious, remind yourself that you know the material. Visualize successfully completing the test. Then take a few deep, relaxing breaths and return to it. Work through the questions carefully but with confidence, knowing that you are capable of succeeding.

Developing a healthy mental approach to test taking will also aid in other areas of life. Test anxiety affects more than just the actual test—it can be damaging to your mental health and even contribute to depression. It's important to beat test anxiety before it becomes a problem for more than testing.

Study Strategy

Being prepared for the test is necessary to combat anxiety, but what does being prepared look like? You may study for hours on end and still not feel prepared. What you need is a strategy for test prep. The next few pages outline our recommended steps to help you plan out and conquer the challenge of preparation.

Step 1: Scope Out the Test

Learn everything you can about the format (multiple choice, essay, etc.) and what will be on the test. Gather any study materials, course outlines, or sample exams that may be available. Not only will this help you to prepare, but knowing what to expect can help to alleviate test anxiety.

Step 2: Map Out the Material

Look through the textbook or study guide and make note of how many chapters or sections it has. Then divide these over the time you have. For example, if a book has 15 chapters and you have five days to study, you need to cover three chapters each day. Even better, if you have the time, leave an extra day at the end for overall review after you have gone through the material in depth.

If time is limited, you may need to prioritize the material. Look through it and make note of which sections you think you already have a good grasp on, and which need review. While you are studying, skim quickly through the familiar sections and take more time on the challenging parts.

Write out your plan so you don't get lost as you go. Having a written plan also helps you feel more in control of the study, so anxiety is less likely to arise from feeling overwhelmed at the amount to cover.

Step 3: Gather Your Tools

Decide what study method works best for you. Do you prefer to highlight in the book as you study and then go back over the highlighted portions? Or do you type out notes of the important information? Or is it helpful to make flashcards that you can carry with you? Assemble the pens, index cards, highlighters, post-it notes, and any other materials you may need so you won't be distracted by getting up to find things while you study.

If you're having a hard time retaining the information or organizing your notes, experiment with different methods. For example, try color-coding by subject with colored pens, highlighters, or post-it notes. If you learn better by hearing, try recording yourself reading your notes so you can listen while in the car, working out, or simply sitting at your desk. Ask a friend to quiz you from your flashcards, or try teaching someone the material to solidify it in your mind.

Step 4: Create Your Environment

It's important to avoid distractions while you study. This includes both the obvious distractions like visitors and the subtle distractions like an uncomfortable chair (or a too-comfortable couch that makes you want to fall asleep). Set up the best study environment possible: good lighting and a comfortable work area. If background music helps you focus, you may want to turn it on, but otherwise keep the room quiet. If you are using a computer to take notes, be sure you don't have any other windows open, especially applications like social media, games, or anything else that could distract you. Silence your phone and turn off notifications. Be sure to keep water close by so you stay hydrated while you study (but avoid unhealthy drinks and snacks).

Also, take into account the best time of day to study. Are you freshest first thing in the morning? Try to set aside some time then to work through the material. Is your mind clearer in the afternoon or evening? Schedule your study session then. Another method is to study at the same time of day that you will take the test, so that your brain gets used to working on the material at that time and will be ready to focus at test time.

Step 5: Study!

Once you have done all the study preparation, it's time to settle into the actual studying. Sit down, take a few moments to settle your mind so you can focus, and begin to follow your study plan. Don't give in to distractions or let yourself procrastinate. This is your time to prepare so you'll be ready to fearlessly approach the test. Make the most of the time and stay focused.

Of course, you don't want to burn out. If you study too long you may find that you're not retaining the information very well. Take regular study breaks. For example, taking five minutes out of every hour to walk briskly, breathing deeply and swinging your arms, can help your mind stay fresh.

As you get to the end of each chapter or section, it's a good idea to do a quick review. Remind yourself of what you learned and work on any difficult parts. When you feel that you've mastered the material, move on to the next part. At the end of your study session, briefly skim through your notes again.

But while review is helpful, cramming last minute is NOT. If at all possible, work ahead so that you won't need to fit all your study into the last day. Cramming overloads your brain with more information than it can process and retain, and your tired mind may struggle to recall even previously learned information when it is overwhelmed with last-minute study. Also, the urgent nature of cramming and the stress placed on your brain contribute to anxiety. You'll be more likely to go to the test feeling unprepared and having trouble thinking clearly.

So don't cram, and don't stay up late before the test, even just to review your notes at a leisurely pace. Your brain needs rest more than it needs to go over the information again. In fact, plan to finish your studies by noon or early afternoon the day before the test. Give your brain the rest of the day to relax or focus on other things, and get a good night's sleep. Then you will be fresh for the test and better able to recall what you've studied.

Step 6: Take a Practice Test

Many courses offer sample tests, either online or in the study materials. This is an excellent resource to check whether you have mastered the material, as well as to prepare for the test format and environment.

Check the test format ahead of time: the number of questions, the type (multiple choice, free response, etc.), and the time limit. Then create a plan for working through them. For example, if you have 30 minutes to take a 60-question test, your limit is 30 seconds per question. Spend less time on the questions you know well so that you can take more time on the difficult ones.

If you have time to take several practice tests, take the first one open book, with no time limit. Work through the questions at your own pace and make sure you fully understand them. Gradually work up to taking a test under test conditions: sit at a desk with all study materials put away and set a timer. Pace yourself to make sure you finish the test with time to spare and go back to check your answers if you have time.

After each test, check your answers. On the questions you missed, be sure you understand why you missed them. Did you misread the question (tests can use tricky wording)? Did you forget the information? Or was it something you hadn't learned? Go back and study any shaky areas that the practice tests reveal.

Taking these tests not only helps with your grade, but also aids in combating test anxiety. If you're already used to the test conditions, you're less likely to worry about it, and working through tests until you're scoring well gives you a confidence boost. Go through the practice tests until you feel comfortable, and then you can go into the test knowing that you're ready for it.

Test Tips

On test day, you should be confident, knowing that you've prepared well and are ready to answer the questions. But aside from preparation, there are several test day strategies you can employ to maximize your performance.

First, as stated before, get a good night's sleep the night before the test (and for several nights before that, if possible). Go into the test with a fresh, alert mind rather than staying up late to study.

Try not to change too much about your normal routine on the day of the test. It's important to eat a nutritious breakfast, but if you normally don't eat breakfast at all, consider eating just a protein bar. If you're a coffee drinker, go ahead and have your normal coffee. Just make sure you time it so that the caffeine doesn't wear off right in the middle of your test. Avoid sugary beverages, and drink enough water to stay hydrated but not so much that you need a restroom break 10 minutes into the test. If your test isn't first thing in the morning, consider going for a walk or doing a light workout before the test to get your blood flowing.

Allow yourself enough time to get ready, and leave for the test with plenty of time to spare so you won't have the anxiety of scrambling to arrive in time. Another reason to be early is to select a good seat. It's helpful to sit away from doors and windows, which can be distracting. Find a good seat, get out your supplies, and settle your mind before the test begins.

When the test begins, start by going over the instructions carefully, even if you already know what to expect. Make sure you avoid any careless mistakes by following the directions.

Then begin working through the questions, pacing yourself as you've practiced. If you're not sure on an answer, don't spend too much time on it, and don't let it shake your confidence. Either skip it and come back later, or eliminate as many wrong answers as possible and guess among the remaining ones. Don't dwell on these questions as you continue—put them out of your mind and focus on what lies ahead.

Be sure to read all of the answer choices, even if you're sure the first one is the right answer. Sometimes you'll find a better one if you keep reading. But don't second-guess yourself if you do immediately know the answer. Your gut instinct is usually right. Don't let test anxiety rob you of the information you know.

If you have time at the end of the test (and if the test format allows), go back and review your answers. Be cautious about changing any, since your first instinct tends to be correct, but make sure you didn't misread any of the questions or accidentally mark the wrong answer choice. Look over any you skipped and make an educated guess.

At the end, leave the test feeling confident. You've done your best, so don't waste time worrying about your performance or wishing you could change anything. Instead, celebrate the successful completion of this test. And finally, use this test to learn how to deal with anxiety even better next time.

Review Video: Test Anxiety
Visit mometrix.com/academy and enter code: 100340

Important Qualification

Not all anxiety is created equal. If your test anxiety is causing major issues in your life beyond the classroom or testing center, or if you are experiencing troubling physical symptoms related to your anxiety, it may be a sign of a serious physiological or psychological condition. If this sounds like your situation, we strongly encourage you to seek professional help.

Online Resources

Due to our efforts to try to keep this book to a manageable length, we've created a link that will give you access to all of your online resources:

mometrix.com/resources719/dsstmoneybank

It's Your Moment, Let's Celebrate It!

Share your story @mometrixtestpreparation